I0755712

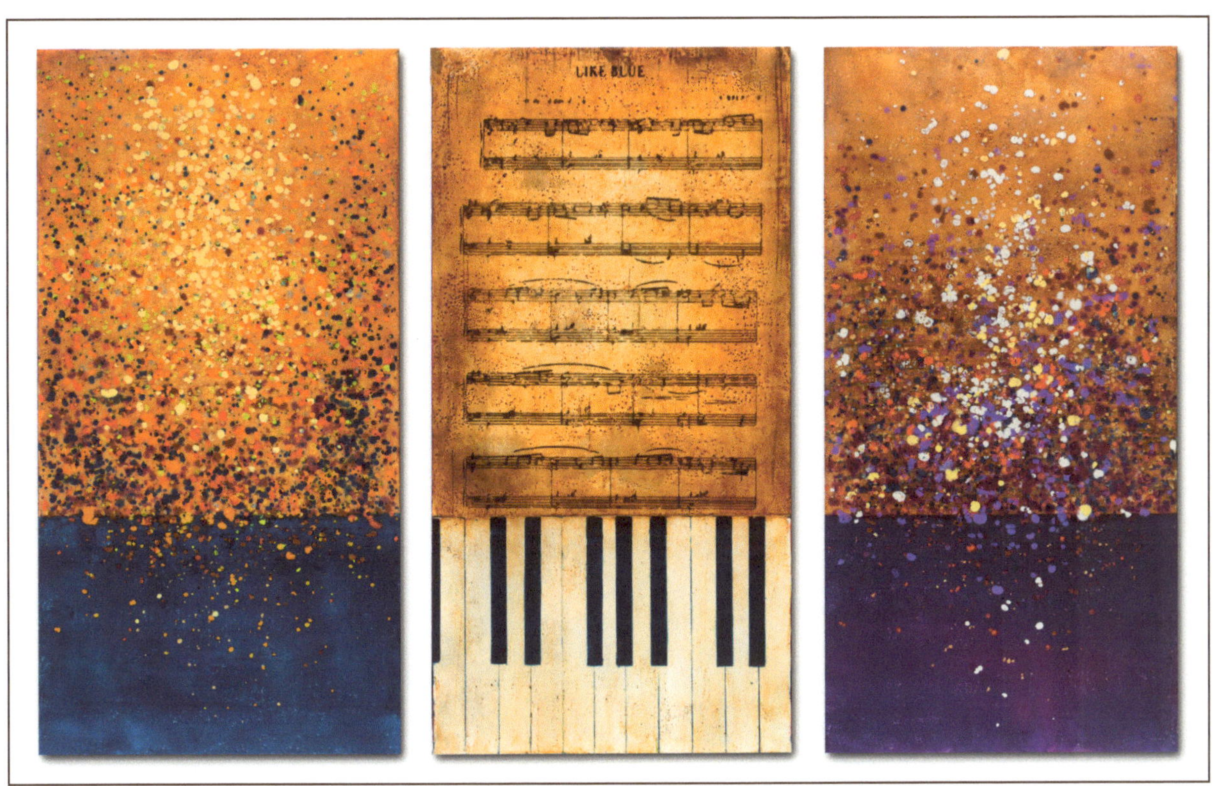


# *Extraordinary* GIFTS

*Remarkable Women of the Delaware Valley*

EDITED BY

Melissa Tevere • Tara S. Smith
Carla Spataro • Courtney Bambrick

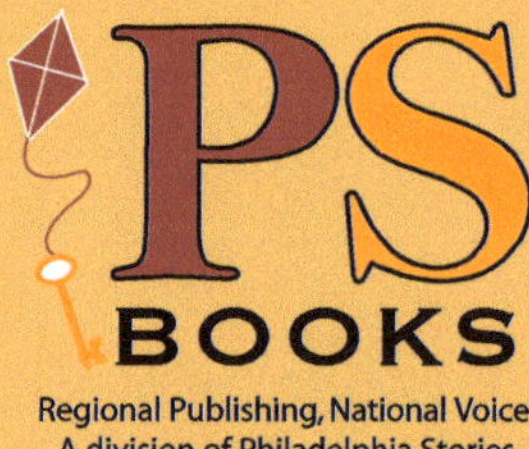


93 Old York Road, Ste. 1-753
Jenkintown, PA 19046
www.psbookspublishing.org



Published by PS Books, a division of Philadelphia Stories, Inc.

ISBN 978-0-9793350-8-2



All proceeds from the sale of this book support Philadelphia Stories, a free nonprofit literary magazine publishing writers and artists from the Delaware Valley.

Book Design by Vignette Visual Media
Cover Image: Suzanne Comer, © 2013
Inside Cover Image: Lisa Basil, © 2013

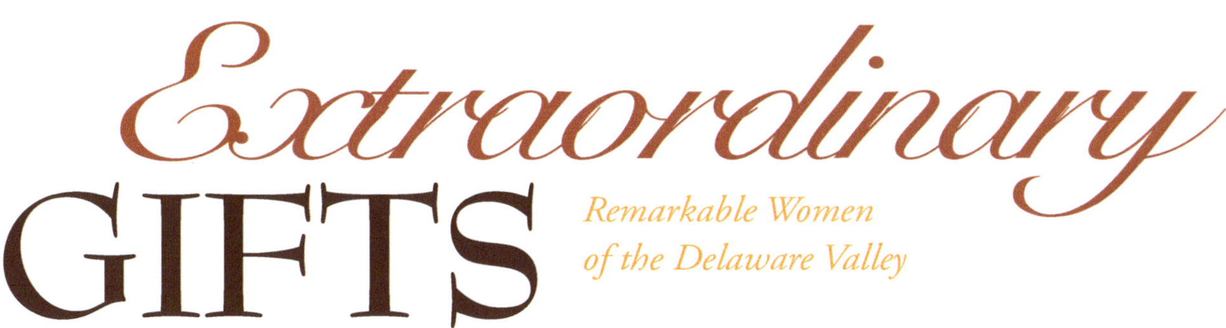


## CONTENTS

# *Extraordinary* GIFTS

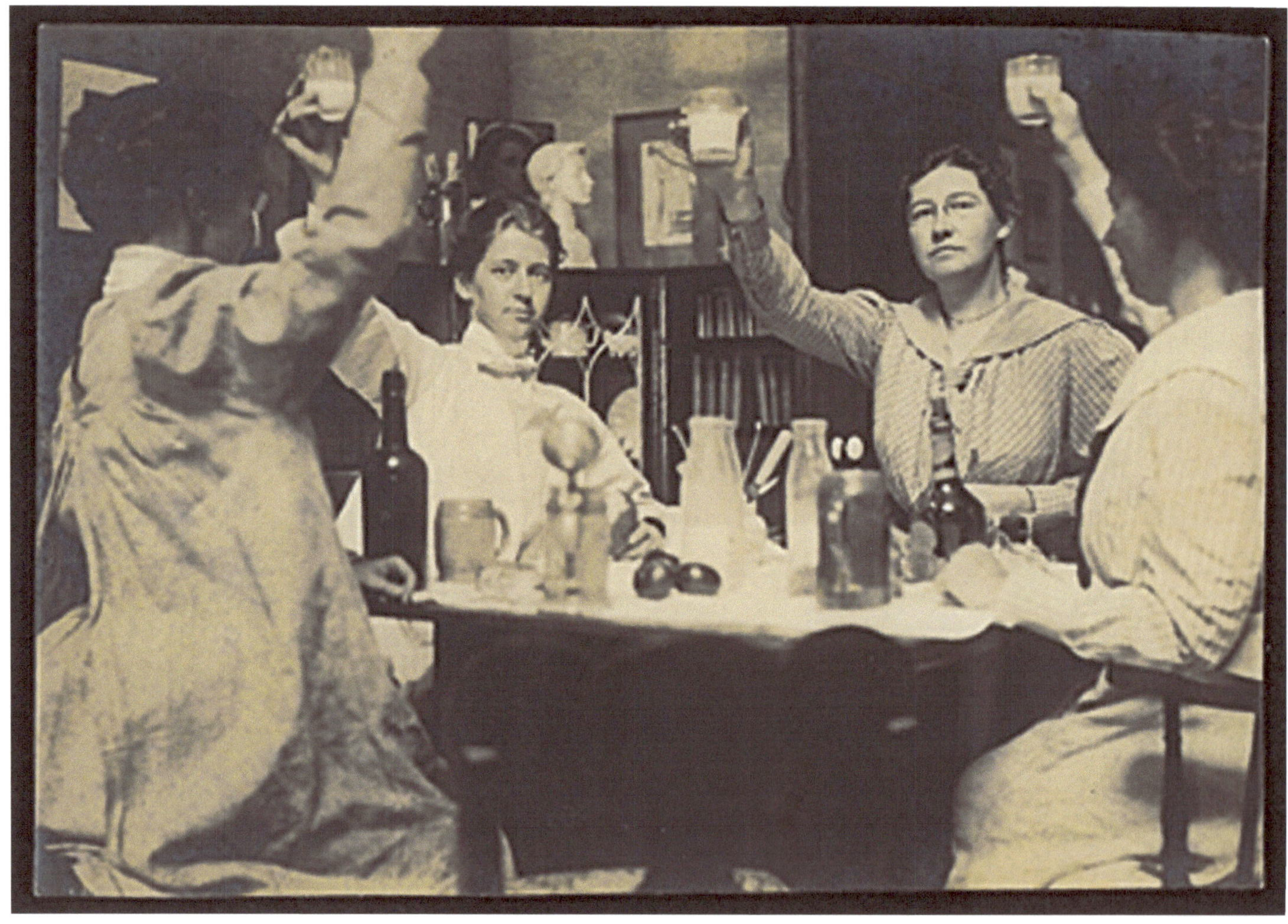

*(Smithsonian Archives of American Art)*

*Violet Oakley, Jessie Willcox Smith, Elizabeth Shippen Green, and Henrietta Cozens (ca. 1901) were known as the Red Rose Girls. The three artists lived together with their friend Henrietta Cozens at the Red Rose Inn in Villanova.* *For more on the Red Rose Girls, see p. 32.*

# INTRODUCTION

> *"Jo, you have so many extraordinary gifts; how can you expect to lead an ordinary life? You're ready to go out and—and find a good use for your talent. ...Go, and embrace your liberty. And see what wonderful things come of it."*
>
> — *Louisa May Alcott,* Little Women, *1869*

Inspired by Jo March and her creator Louisa May Alcott, and by countless other women who have gone before, generations of girls have grown up to change the world through their courage to think outside the box and to go against convention. *Extraordinary Gifts* celebrates twenty women who have, like Jo, "embraced their liberty" by using their extraordinary gifts to lead extraordinary lives.

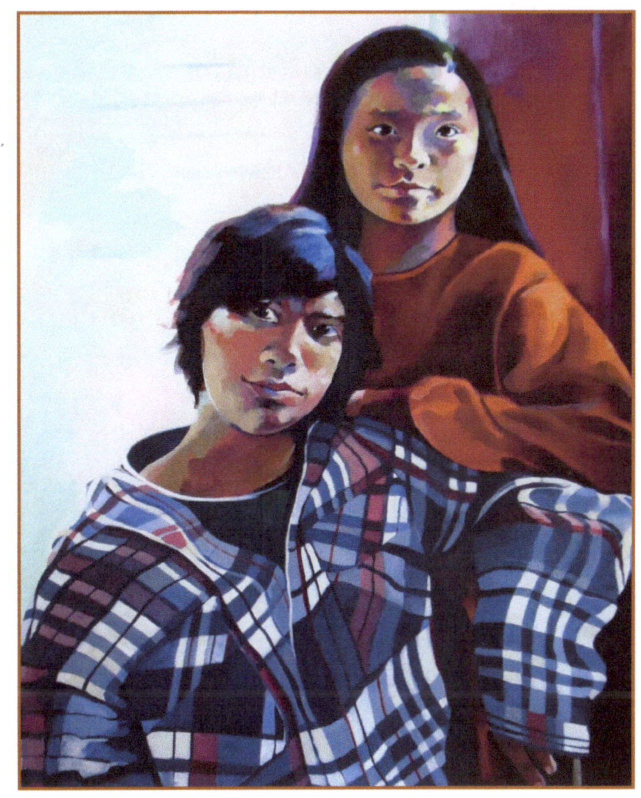

Artist's Children *by Melissa Tevere*

One of these women is painter Alice Neel (1900–1984), my own personal hero. Like Alice, I am a painter and a single mom. Painting is part of my everyday. My paints and easel are set up in my kitchen so that I can help my two children with their homework and make dinner as I work. Alice lived her adult life in New York City and raised two boys in much the same way—she lived in a small apartment and wove creating art into the fabric of their everyday life. My connection to Alice Neel deepened when I learned that she grew up in Colwyn, Pennsylvania, close to where I was raised in

Springfield, Delaware County. I started to wonder—what other remarkable women shared my Philadelphia and Delaware Valley roots?

I could never have envisioned the breadth of beauty, courage, and creativity I would discover in answer to this question. *Extraordinary Gifts* combines visual art with poems and short fiction inspired by twenty remarkable women who paved the way for the female writers, poets, and artists featured in this exhibition and book. Some of these women—Louisa May Alcott, Margaret Mead, and Marian Anderson among them—are well known. Others, such as Alice Steer Wilson, Dorothy P. Miller, and Helga Testorf, might be less familiar. None of them, however, allowed the limitations of society's expectations for their gender to stop them from fulfilling their potential.

While every woman builds on the legacy of women from previous generations, the poem inspired by Alice Steer Wilson (1927–2001), a painter and arts educator from Cape May, New Jersey, was written by her daughter, Janice Wilson Stridick (see p. 63). Stridick reflects:

> *... this poem epitomizes my journey into my mother's studio after she died ... she had never revealed this wonderful, strong, unfinished self-portrait, which she had painted after her first battle with breast cancer. She had straight black hair, but in this painting, her hair was curly as it grew back after chemotherapy. The portrait is dramatic and confrontational—she looks directly at the viewer with an unapologetic, serious gaze. When I first saw it, I felt she was aware that her time was short, but her legacy would be long ... [it conveyed] to me a sense of self-awareness and strength, in the face of dismissal or skepticism.*

All of the women in these pages persevered in the face of dismissal and skepticism, including Ruth Robinhold (1913–2012), who laughed in the face of opposition and just kept rowing. Ruth was one of the founders of the Philadelphia Girls' Rowing Club on Boathouse Row. In 1938, defying an

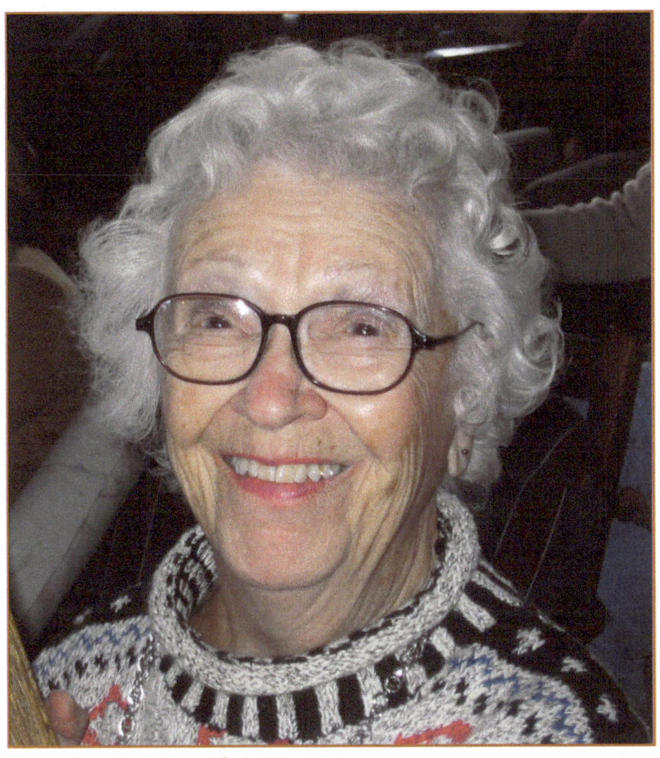

Ruth Robinhold *(© Dona File, PGRC, 2011)*

*Everyone stopped and stared at me. "Are you kidding? That's Ruthie Robinhold! She's the reason women first got the chance to row in Philadelphia."*

*"Is she serious?" I asked. "She wants to go drinking with us?"*

*They laughed.*
*"Oh, just you wait and see!"*

**all-male Schuylkill River skulling tradition, she boldly advertised in the local paper for women to join her competitive rowing club. Photographer Michelle Ciarlo-Hayes was training and racing at the Undine Barge Club (next to the PGRC) in 2001 when an octogenarian called to her teammates from the next dock over, inviting herself to drinks and dinner. Michelle asked who the woman was. Ruth did indeed join them for drinks, and dinner, and Michelle enjoyed hearing some of this extraordinary woman's story (see p. 52). She also learned, she says,**

*... never to assume that because someone is sixty-five years older than you that they can't keep up at the bar. "A hand without a drink is like flying with one wing," Ruth said to me that night. "It just doesn't make sense."*

**How I wish, as I look through this book, that I could spend time with each of these women over dinner and drinks, hearing their stories as Michelle did with Ruth. These women encourage us all to live fearlessly, to dare greatly, to share our "extraordinary gifts." Without the legacy of these bold women, it would be like flying with one wing. It just wouldn't make sense.**

— Melissa Borko Tevere

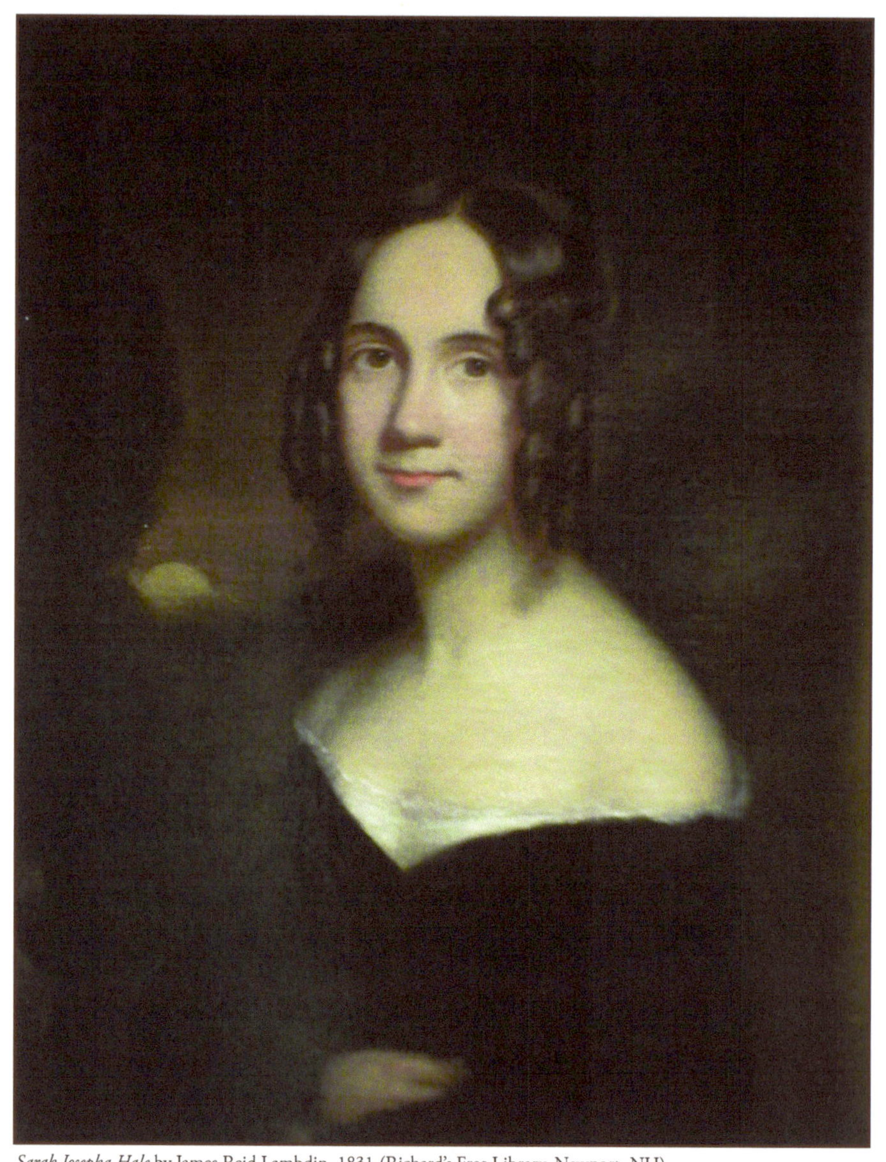

*Sarah Josepha Hale* by James Reid Lambdin, 1831 (Richard's Free Library, Newport, NH)

*"I owe my early predilection for literary pursuits to the teaching and example of my mother. She had enjoyed uncommon advantages of education for a female of her times."*

*~ Sarah Josepha Hale,* The Ladies' Wreath, *1837*

(1788-1879)

# Sarah Josepha Hale

*Writer and Magazine Editor*

*Though young children still sing Sarah Hale's "Mary had a Little Lamb," her legacy as writer, editor, and activist extends far beyond a nursery rhyme. Hale wrote more than fifty books (novels, poetry, and nonfiction) and was the editor of two national women's magazines at a time when few women reached such heights in the publishing industry. She also advocated for higher education for women—which was considered radical in the nineteenth century.*

*Born on a small New Hampshire farm, Hale received little formal education. Beyond what she learned from her mother and what her brother taught her when he came home from college at Dartmouth, she was an autodidact. She and her husband, David Hale, formed a small literary club in 1813. When David died in 1822, Hale was pregnant with their fifth child. She relied on writing to support herself and her two daughters and three sons. Hale's novel* Northwood *was well received, and in 1827 she was hired as editor of the Boston-based* Ladies' Magazine.

*Her work attracted the attention of Louis Godey, who persuaded Hale to move to Philadelphia to be the editor (she preferred the title "editress") of* Godey's Lady's Book. *She remained at Godey's for forty years. Hale insisted on publishing original work in the magazine, and much of it was geared towards the education of women. She gave a voice to American writers including Edgar Allen Poe, Henry Wadsworth Longfellow, Nathaniel Hawthorne, and Emma Willard.* Godey's Lady's Book *had the widest circulation of any magazine of its day and is best known today for the hand-tinted fashion plates that appeared in each issue.*

*Hale used her position of influence to write in defense of causes as various as education, exercise, and sensible fashion for women; household economy; the American union; and the emancipation of slaves. Hale was particularly instrumental in the establishment of Vassar College, which opened in 1861. While Hale championed education for women, she believed that they should use this education to teach or work in the medical field. A woman's primary place, she maintained, was in the home.*

— Nicole Contosta

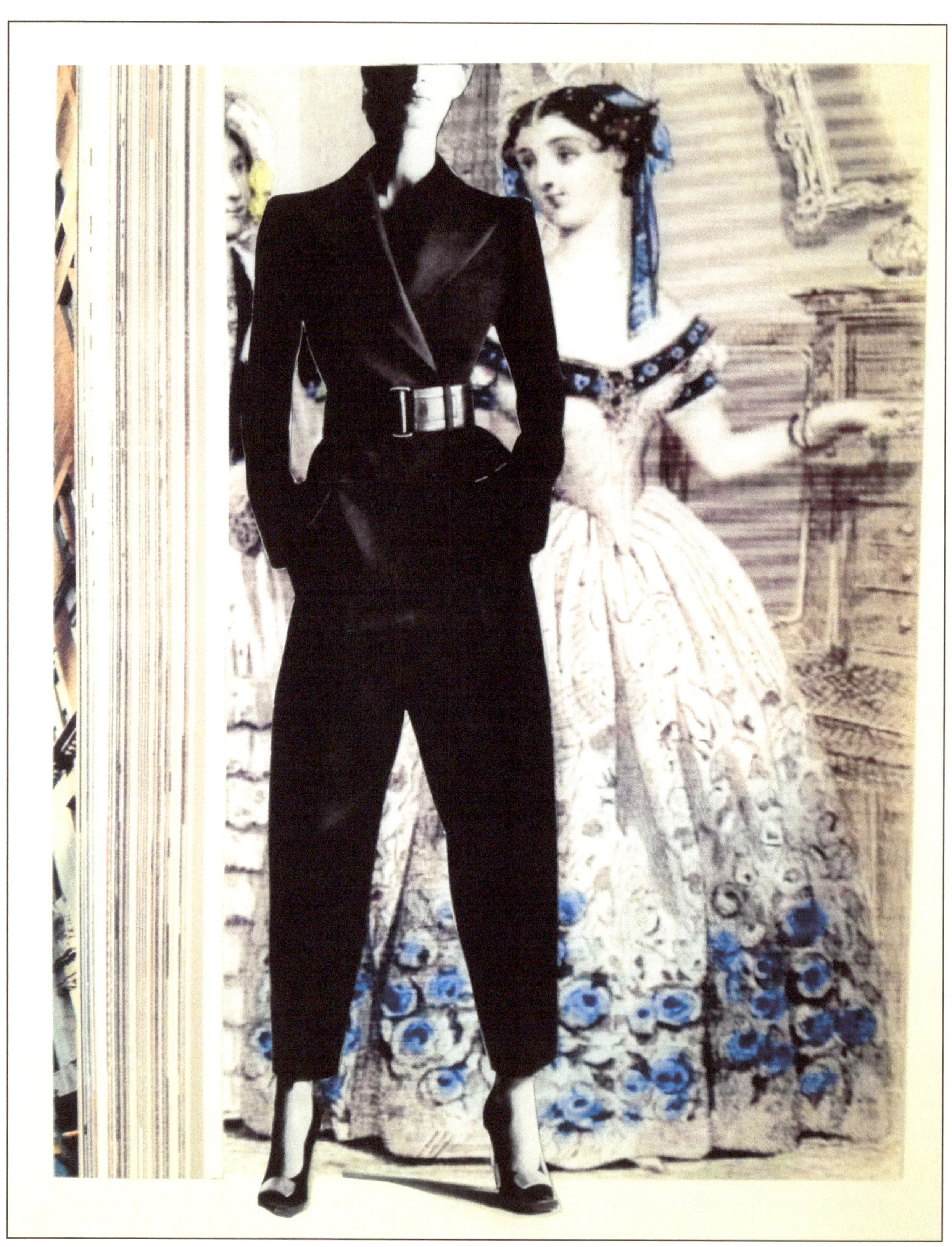

Felise Luchansky
*Prevailing Fashions I – IV*, collage, 16" x 13"

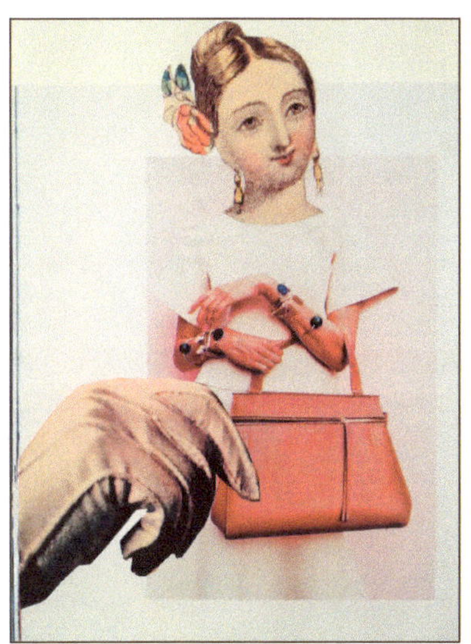

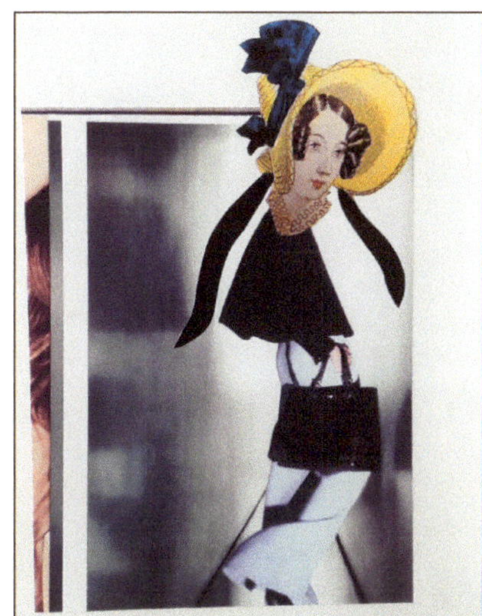

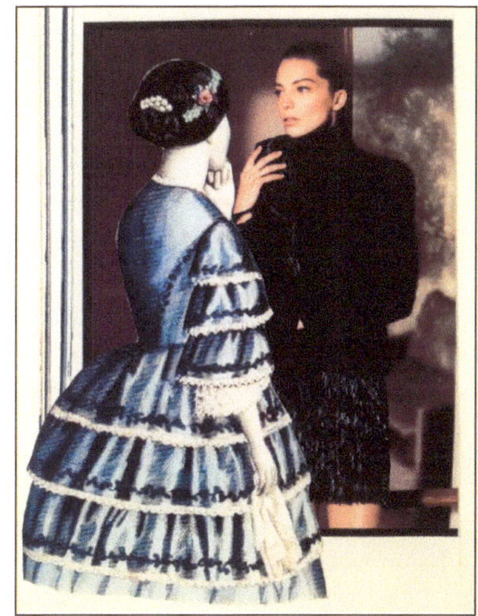

# SARAH'S DAUGHTERS

Tara S. Smith

## 1982

My mother had heard, on EAZY 101 or in the Campbell's soup aisle at Pantry Pride, that some mother somewhere had made a sign, "Mom on Strike," dragged a chair onto her lawn, and sat down. This news, instead of peanut butter on celery sticks, greeted us fresh off the bus. "I'm sick and tired," she said, "and I'm going on strike." She'd made a list, instead of a sign. So we three picked up—socks, projects, dog poop. Our fighting—*bickering*—was part of the big stink, but we'd never felt such solidarity. We raised our eyebrows, tiptoed, whispered. Will it be over by dinner, my brother wanted to know. She sat in the living room doing nothing. She seemed different. Resolute. Outside, I gathered bikes, balls, hula hoops—*debris*—and my younger sister wielded the pooper scooper. Over the hedge, the silent suburbanscape of neighbor lawns reassured us. It wasn't an epidemic. It was just our mother. "Wait til Dad gets home," I said.

When my father got home he scrambled eggs, scooped ice cream, sent us to bed. In the morning he announced that our mother was going to work. "She does work," I corrected him. "She's a domestic engineer."

"Outside the home," he said.

"What about us?" I asked.

"What about you," he said. "Get ready for school."

"Working will help me be a better wife and mother," she explained later.

"We'll be products of a broken home!" I wailed. My father looked at me. "I mean latchkey kids," I said.

Things went from bad to worse—child sitters, chore charts, Hamburger Helper. The broken home came later.

## 2013

Dancing my toddler daughter round the room, I sang: "Mommy got a job, Mommy got a job, Mommy's a stay-at-home freelance mom!" She giggled, brushed her bangs out of her eyes, clapped. "Hi-ho, the derry-o!" That was Monday. Tuesday was for tantrums, jellied crumbs stuck in her hair. "No job! No more job!"

That was years ago. Today my friend is over at Bibliophile, guest blogging, sallying around the internet like it's a cocktail party. I'm at my kitchen table with a sick cat, a project to finish, and a deadline, googling, "Is there a union for stay-at-home emptying nester freelance moms tired of picking up and nagging?" Nearly four thousand results, not one answer.

## 1982

My A+ report entitled "Sarah Josepha Hale: Magnificent Matriarch of Thanksgiving" in hand, I rose at the dinner table to read. Sarah Hale told President Lincoln to pick one day for Thanksgiving, I explained. A widow with five kids, she wrote books and edited magazines. I paused. "Sarah also predicated that women should stay home because being a mother is their paramount job. The end." My mother studied her casserole. "That's where my thesaurus went," my father said. "I will never abandon my children," I declared.

## 2013

My son texts me from the basement: What's for dinner. Cursor pulses, time warps, Hestia flickers. I want to escape. I want to strike. I want, too late, to ask my mother more about it. I make dinner.

*"As it is desirable that man should act a manly and generous part, not 'mannish,' so let woman be urged to exercise a dignified and womanly bearing, not womanish. Let her cultivate all the graces and proper accomplishments of her sex, but let not these degenerate into a kind of effeminacy, in which she is satisfied to be the mere plaything or toy of society, content with her outward adornings, and with the tone of flattery and fulsome adulation too often addressed to her."*

~ *Lucretia Mott,* Discourse on Woman, *1849*

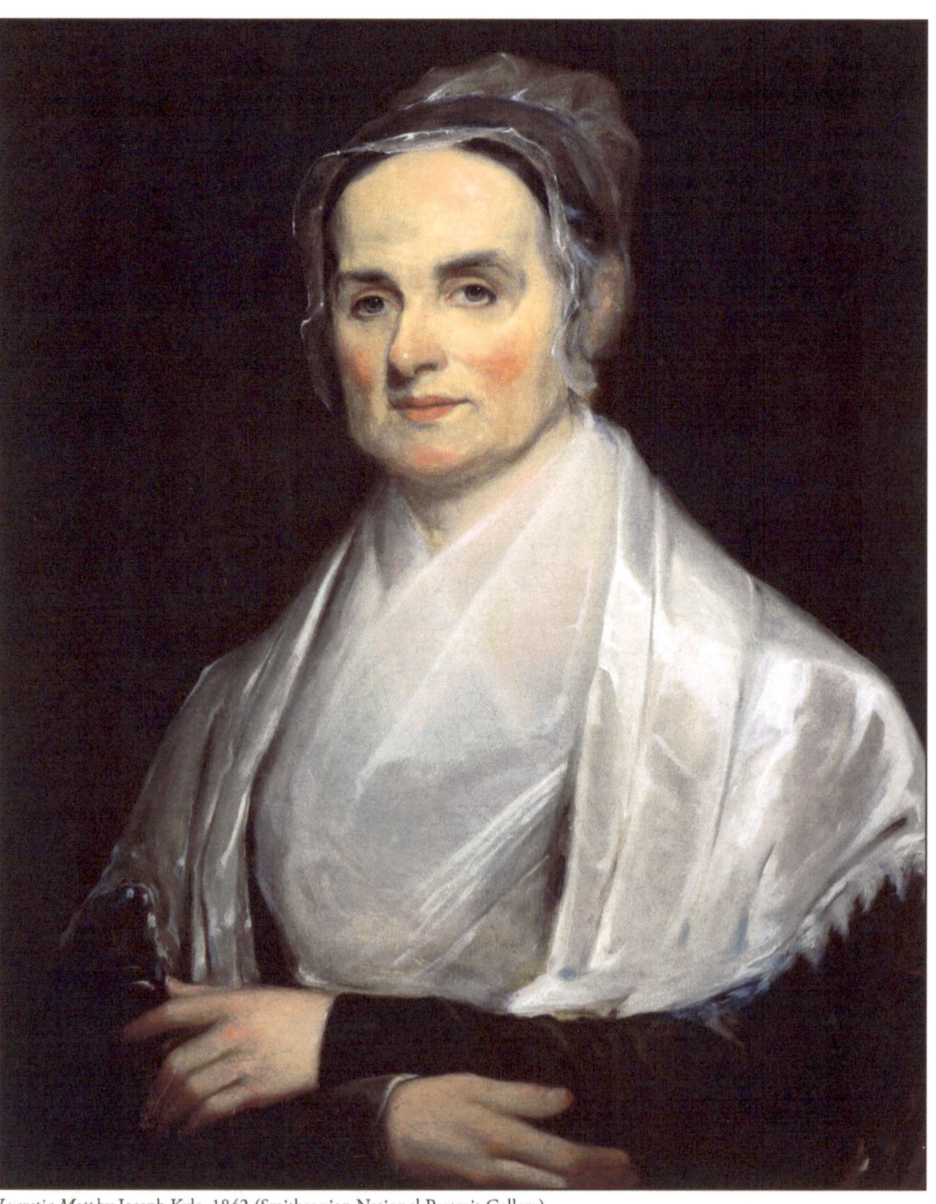

*Lucretia Mott* by Joseph Kyle, 1842 (Smithsonian National Portrait Gallery)

(1793-1880)

# Lucretia Mott

*Abolitionist*

*Lucretia Mott was born to a Quaker family in Nantucket, Massachusetts in 1793. When she was thirteen years old, Mott attended Nine Partners Quaker Boarding School in New York. While there she learned about slavery and was filled with indignation when she discovered that the male teachers at the school earned three times as much as the female teachers. Mott devoted herself to working to right social injustice from a young age.*

*She married James Mott in 1811. The couple settled in Philadelphia and had six children. Despite suffering the tragedy of losing a child, Mott never faltered in her faith. In 1821 she became a Quaker minister, but her strong opposition to slavery and her support of William Lloyd Garrison and the American Anti-Slavery Society made her a target for threats and controversy. She was a skilled public speaker and spoke out for abolition. She also sheltered runaway slaves in her Philadelphia home.*

*Mott attended the World's Anti-Slavery Convention in London in 1840, but the organization did not allow women to attend as full participants. This discrimination pushed Mott and her new friend, Elizabeth Cady Stanton, to action. Mott and Stanton began to work for women's rights in the United States and organized the Seneca Falls Convention (the first women's rights convention) in New York in 1848.*

*In 1849 Mott published a speech about the restrictions of gender,* Discourse on Woman, *as a pamphlet. She continued to be a dedicated activist for the women's rights movement and, at the end of the Civil War, was elected as the first president of the American Equal Rights Association. Mott worked tirelessly to secure the rights of African Americans as well as the rights of women and also helped found Swarthmore College in 1864. Mott leaves an inspiring legacy as a social reformer and as a leader in both the abolition and suffrage movements.*

— Rachel Mamola

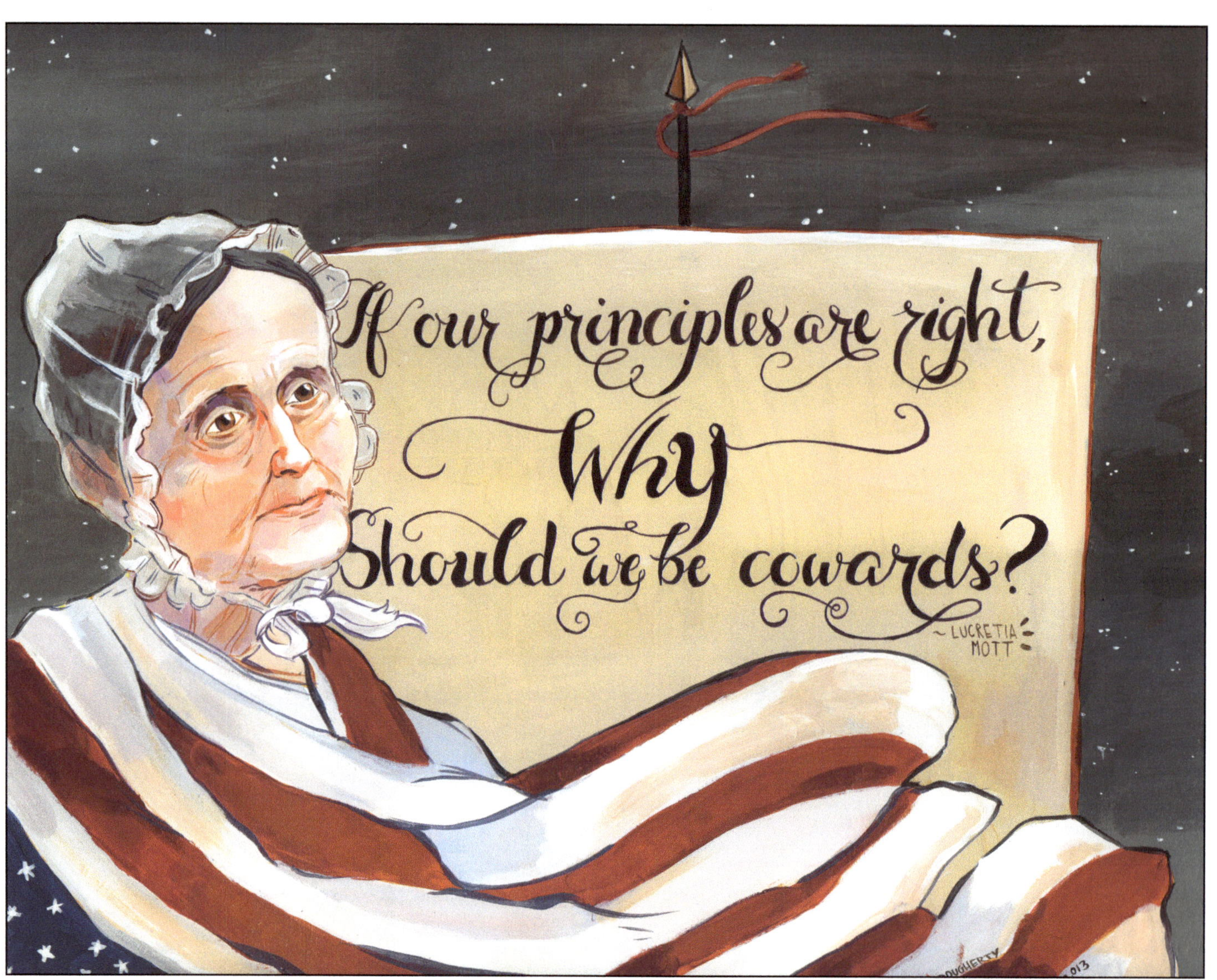


Rachel Dougherty
*La Mott,* acrylic on wood panel, 16" x 20"

Lucretia Mott

# THIS TYPE

Alyesha Wise

I have not always stood this type of woman
I had to crawl on unequal ground
Before walking into myself
I did not pass up love on the journey
Exercising this heart with my husband's touch
Was a reminder that the entire world isn't held up
Or down
By the senseless
And the blind
Who choose not to respect hierarchy in a skirt
Or human in darker hue

I have not always stood this strong a Quaker
I had to listen to fools speak before no longer listening to fools speak
Listening
Is a remarkable skill
Shouting *Enough is enough!*
Is even more remarkable
It takes a whole lot of courage
And a spine with each vertebra replaced with *No*
*No!*
I will not cloak in your cotton
Taste the blood of sugar cane upon my tongue
I will not button my lips
Or my shirt
For you to listen to my opinion
I will minister my words until the moon is full
And the dim-lit sun remembers why it stands
Until gravity no longer permits me to hold the weight of the blacks
And the women
And my children
To the heights of Heaven
I will ALWAYS stand this type of woman
So that even when I am gone
The lies from a fool's lips cannot hinder a soul
No labor can weaken a warrior
And the divinity within all of us
Will never be forgotten

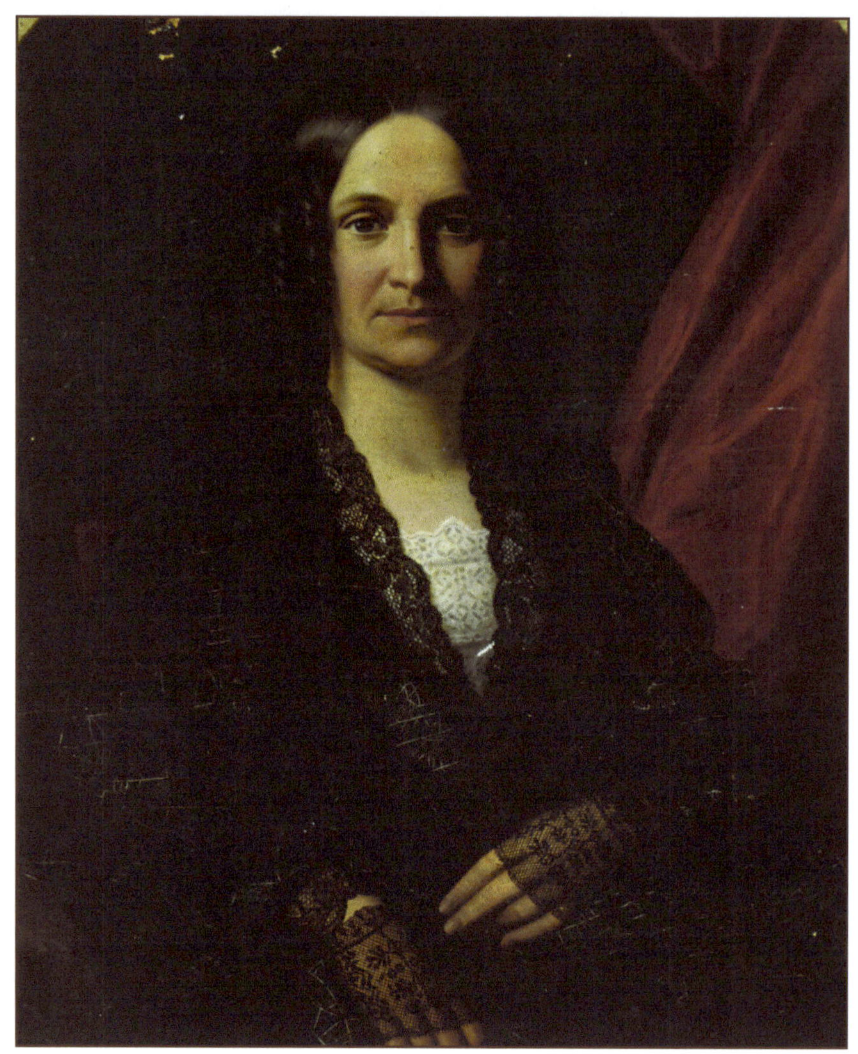

*Sarah Worthington King Peter*, ca. 1840–1845
(Courtesy of the Ohio Historical Society, Catalog No. AL04649)

*"Having for a number of years observed with deep concern the privation and suffering to which a large and increasing number of deserving women are exposed in this city and elsewhere for want of a wider scope in which to earn their living; . . . I resolved to attempt the instruction of a class of young girls in the practice of such of the arts of design as were within my reach."*

*~ letter to the Franklin Institute's Board of Managers, March 27, 1850*

# (1800–1877)

## Sarah Worthington Peter

*Founder, Moore College of Art and Design*

*Sarah Worthington, the beautiful and educated daughter of Ohio governor and U.S. Senator Thomas Worthington, married Edward King at the age of sixteen. When Edward died in 1836, the young widow brought her two sons to Cambridge to complete their education at Harvard College. Friends in their Boston circle included Daniel Webster, James Russell Lowell, Washington Irving, and the young Longfellow.*

*Her sons' education complete, Worthington was staying with friends in Philadelphia when she met William Peter, a widower serving as British Consul to Pennsylvania and New Jersey. They were married in 1844, and the new Mrs. Peter devoted herself to hospitality and to various philanthropic endeavors. Many of Philadelphia's influential citizens, writers, musicians, and visitors from around the world gathered at their home on Spruce and Third streets.*

*Having long been concerned by "the privation and suffering to which a large and increasing number of women are exposed in this city and elsewhere for want of a wider scope in which to earn their living," Worthington Peter opened the third floor of her home as a school to teach women to design and produce "articles for domestic use and adornment"—from wallpaper to utensils and furniture carving. This School of Design for Women soon outgrew her home, and she sought to affiliate with the Franklin Institute. The officers agreed, provided that she could raise enough money to make it feasible. Her friend Sarah Josepha Hale* *(see p. 8)**, the influential editor of* Godey's Lady's Book*, took up Worthington Peter's cause in 1850 with an appeal for benefactors in the magazine. Fredrika Bremer, a Swedish author and social reformer, wrote that she found Worthington Peter "a warm-hearted, lively lady, particularly zealous on the subject of the development of her sex to a more independent life, both as regards body and soul."*

*In 1850 the school moved to 70 Walnut Street and grew from there to occupy a larger building on the corner of Broad and Master streets in 1881. The school merged with the Moore Institute of Art, Science, and Industry in 1932. Today, the Moore College of Art and Design has an enrollment of nearly five hundred women in its BFA program.*

*Throughout her later years Worthington Peter travelled widely throughout Europe and amassed important collections now housed in the Cincinnati Museum of Art. Following the deaths of her son (in 1850) and her husband (in 1853), Worthington Peter moved back to Cincinnati. There she founded the Ladies' Academy of Fine Arts, which became the Cincinnati Academy of Fine Arts. After her conversion to Roman Catholicism in 1854, she was responsible for opening many schools and hospitals and cared for wounded soldiers during the Civil War. She died in 1877, while making preparations for her seventh trip to Europe.*

— Tara S. Smith

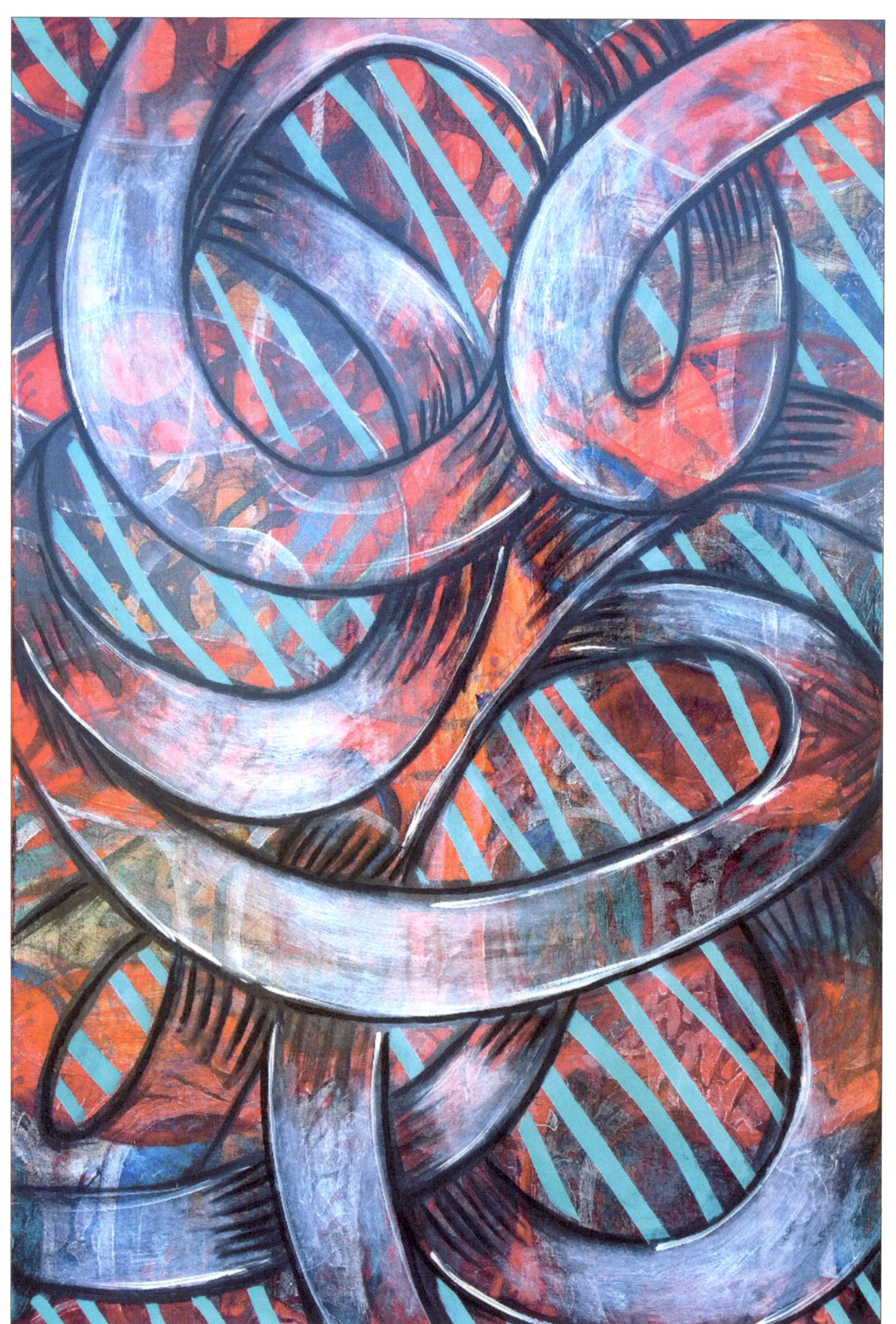

Lisa T. Reed
*Warp & Weft,* acrylic and oil on canvas, 36" x 24"

Sarah Worthington Peter

# LEAP YEAR

Tamara Oakman

In Washington, DC,
a monument of granite and sandstone
sinks its marble roots into the ground.
Somewhere in California, J.W. Marshall

unpeels gold flake surprises from a mill,
and in London, Marx and Engels
set fervor to paper.
My father, a senator, is beautiful as elk.

His stout antlers stand up and branch out
as strange trees. Like with him,
revolution is a two-tailed comet
breaking orbit, taking over the sky.

In the spare holding of my copious house,
I founded Philadelphia School of Design for Women,
lay blankets across tired shoulders,
warm hands with gentle fire.

The Word says, from faith, hope, and charity;
the greatest of these is charity.
In all things charity.
Charity for the widows, the little orphans—

their tiny hands—
and the women—the single women
working with water, but no flour for bread.
These women—in need of Moore.

My wealth, a warm blanket at 77,
is large enough to envelope many.
They culture skills to thrive
as bright as pink flowers on cacti.

And in the end, I dip my stout antlers
down into the deep-sea cosmos—
death be not proud—
but like our morning star, I rise again.
The lies from a fool's lips cannot hinder a soul
No labor can weaken a warrior
And the divinity within all of us
Will never be forgotten

*"We all have our own life to pursue, our own kind of dream to be weaving, and we all have the power to make wishes come true, as long as we keep believing."*

*~ Louisa May Alcott*

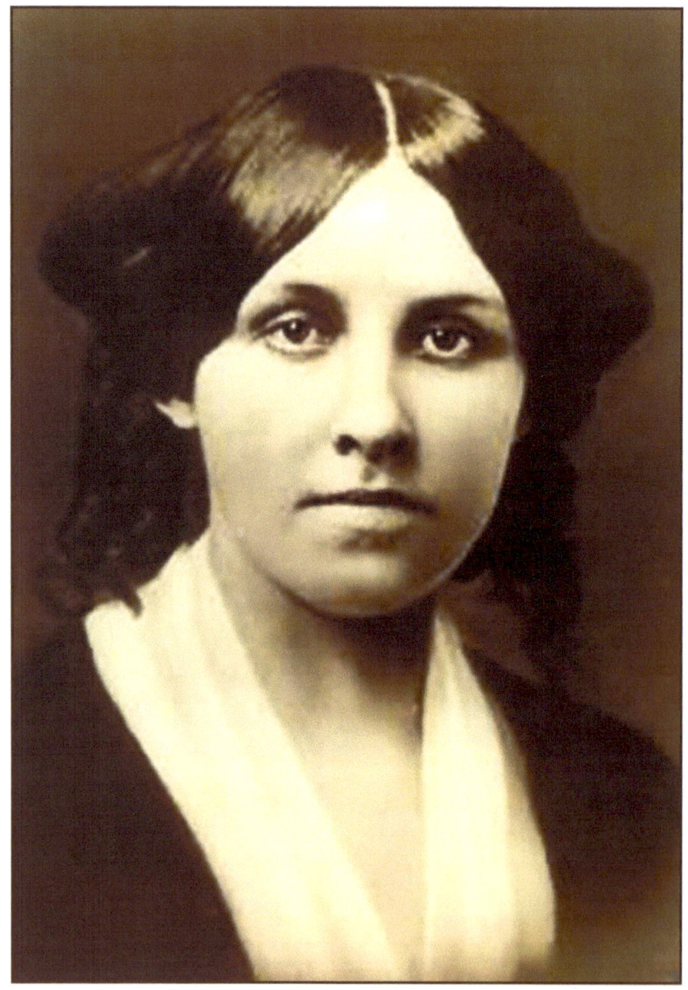

*Louisa May Alcott,* ca. 1857

(1832–1888)

# Louisa May Alcott

*Writer*

*Louisa May Alcott—novelist, short story writer, playwright, and poet—was born in Germantown, Pennsylvania on her father's thirty-third birthday in 1832. When her family moved to Boston, Alcott's father educated her at home and at the Temple School, which he established. Since her parents were transcendentalists, Alcott grew up knowing, and even studying under, transcendentalists and writers including Henry David Thoreau, Ralph Waldo Emerson, and Theodore Parker.*

*Alcott's father founded several schools, but all of them failed. Alcott worked as a teacher, seamstress, domestic servant, and eventually as a writer to contribute to the family finances. She began writing when she was sixteen and published her first poem, under the pseudonym Flora Fairfield, in* Peterson's Magazine *in 1851. Under the name A. M. Barnard, she went on to publish several popular, sensational stories that helped to provide a steady income.*

*In 1862, Alcott went to Washington, DC to serve as a nurse for American Civil War soldiers. Her service was cut short when she contracted typhoid and had to return home. She published her letters, in a volume titled* Hospital Sketches, *in 1863. After the publication of her first novel,* Moods, *in 1864, she travelled to Europe to write and later accepted an editorial job at the American journal* Merry's Museum.

*The novel* Little Women, *published in two parts in 1868 and 1869, established Alcott's career as a writer and changed the face of young adult literature. Alcott drew inspiration from her own life and family relationships for the novel. Critics attribute the lasting appeal of* Little Women *to Alcott's strong characters, including her heroine Jo March. Alcott followed* Little Women *with a series of sequels: the second volume of* Little Women, *titled* Good Wives; Little Men *(1871);* Aunt Jo's Scrap Bag, *a series released between 1872 and 1882; and* How They Turned Out *(1886).* Little Women *earned Alcott widespread fame and more than enough money to support herself and her family.*

*Alcott never fully recovered from her bout with typhoid and, although she continued to write, her health continued to deteriorate. She wrote two novels featuring driven, career-oriented, unmarried female leads—*A Story of Experience *(1873) and* Rose in Bloom *(1876). Critics laud these works for their strong sense of feminism. Alcott also wrote poetry, including "The Lay of the Golden Goose," "A Little Grey Curl," and "A.B.A.," and plays, including* Bianca, Captive of Castile, *and* The Unloved Wife.

*Louisa May Alcott died in Boston in 1888, only hours after her father's death. Her legacy, as one of the most celebrated female authors of all time, lives on.*

— Kara Cochran

# Louisa May Alcott

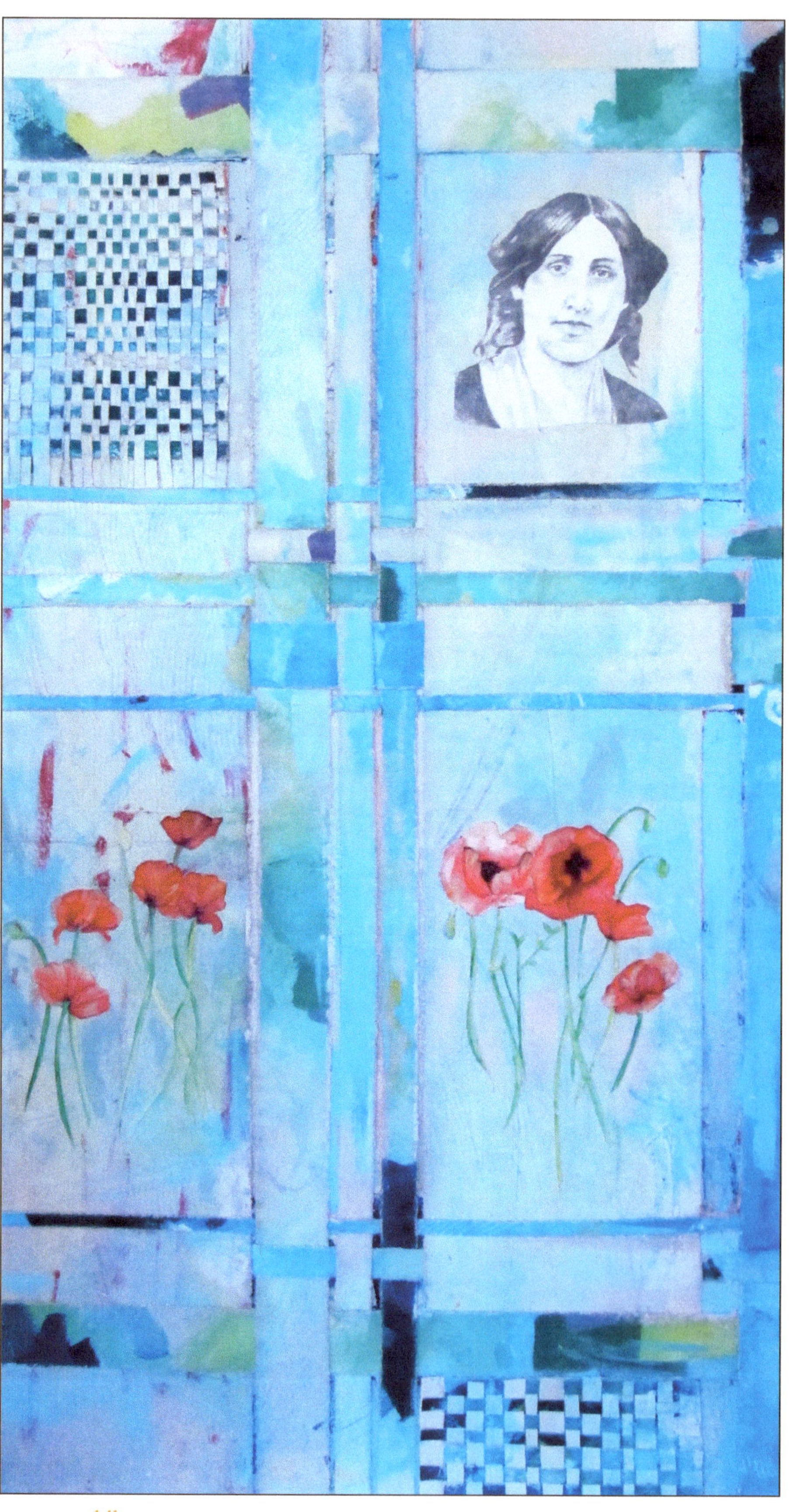

Jessica Padilla
*Untitled,* mixed media on woven canvas, 48" x 26"

# WHAT WAS BURNED

Nancy Kern

That day at the rest home on Dunreath, when the fever seared your body and the divine gavel pressed upon your forehead, you knew it was time for you to decide. You had smelled the mist before: when Lizzie went, begging for ether, when Abba left, calling you mother and talking of soft pillows, when the soldiers asked you to scribe letters to their mothers and wives and daughters. Now, it skulked among the folds of the damask curtains, with a fragrance like the wildflowers Marmee used to keep in the green and white china vase she received on her wedding day. Father beckoned, luminous in the corner. "Is it not meningitis?" you asked, and you lay there, vacillating, waiting for Dr. Lawrence, feeling like Phineas Gage, or perhaps, the way Ms. Dickinson felt when she knew a poem was a poem. The nurses wrung their liver-marked hands.

You called yourself the oyster. Father called you the owl.

Oyster, owl, you ran. You were always the fastest woman in Concord. Sometimes when you ran, you went barefoot, along streams that sang with wedged rocks, up dirt paths that curved like indecision. A heavy heart needs to be coaxed into beating; veins wearied with privation and labor need to be warmed by something, anything at all, to keep the body from throwing itself upon the tracks or drowning in the pond. This almost happened once, long ago. You found yourself listening day after day as the train rumbled just yards behind your clapboard house, as the geese came in for landings upon the water across the road. It would have been so easy, to walk straight into the hands of God, forwards or back, wouldn't it have, but then one afternoon there was a knock at the door, and, opening it, you found a child holding a seedling, roots wrapped in burlap. Her legs were ashy and her hair was nappy, but her dress was pressed and white. *This is for you,* the child said. *You helped my father. You found him in your kitchen and taught him letters.* When you looked at the child's obsidian eyes, you remembered the runaway slave your family had taken in when you were seven. His had been the one and only birth you'd ever witnessed, the grown man emerging from your mother's oven, eyes as black as the cast-iron itself. *I remember*, you said to the girl, *I am glad he survived*, and you took the sapling from her tiny hands and planted it next to the clothesline. You told yourself that if it lived, you would too. It lived, so you decided to take fate by the throat and shake a living out of her.

Little women. Dreadful boys. Blood and thunder. Beautiful truths. The maelstrom of your mind searched for solace in words. There was never enough ink in your inkwell, never enough paper in your house. When your right hand blistered, you taught yourself to use the left. Even in your sleep your mouth would move.

At the rest home on that night when you made your last decision—for it was yours, not the Eternal Maker's or your father's—there was no more need for words. Afterwards, the nurses burned your bedsheets, and your sister stayed up all night, reading your letters and journals, sorting them into two piles, one for Mrs. Cheney, and one to ignite in a pit out back. We will never know which fire was hotter, which flames licked the March air more passionately. We will never know the color of your blood or the perfection of your flaws. That night, the *Times* called your illness "nervous prostration," noting that your death was a double sorrow as you followed your father to the grave. That night, all of Concord smelled the smoke.

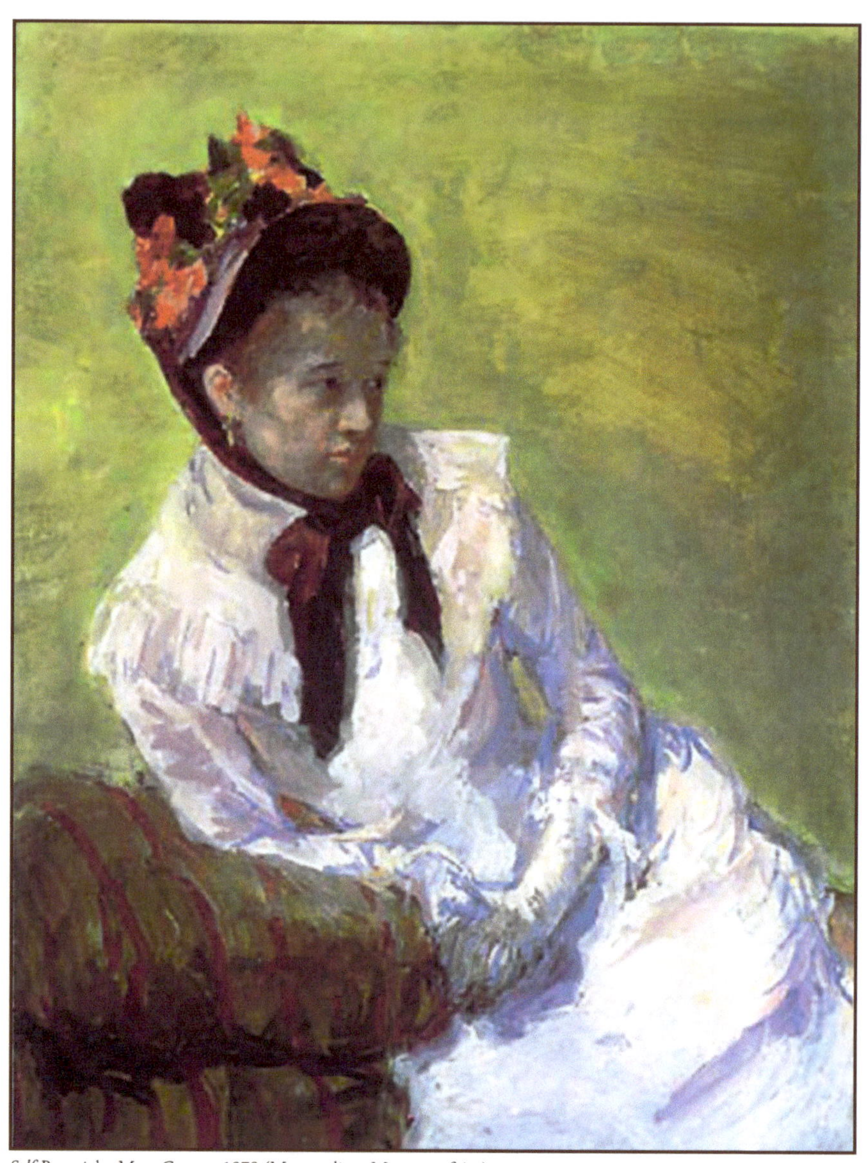

*Self Portrait* by Mary Cassatt, 1878 (Metropolitan Museum of Art)

*"If painting is no longer needed, it seems a shame that some of us are born into the world with such a passion for line and color."*

*~ Mary Cassatt*

(1844-1926)

# Mary Cassatt

*Impressionist Painter*

*Mary Cassatt was born in Allegheny City, Pennsylvania (now part of Pittsburgh) in 1844. Her family lived abroad for several years and she first studied drawing and music as a child in Europe. Her early exposure to French artists at the World's Fair in Paris in 1855 inspired her to pursue a career in art. At age fifteen Cassatt enrolled at the Pennsylvania Academy of the Fine Arts in Philadelphia to study painting, but due to the limited opportunities offered to female art students she decided to study the work of the Old Masters on her own.*

*In 1865 Cassatt travelled again, in spite of her family's objections, and eventually settled in Paris to study privately under Jean-Leon Gerome and Charles Chaplin. Her painting* The Mandolin Player *was accepted by the prestigious Paris Salon in 1868.*

*Edgar Degas, whom Cassatt admired and with whom she developed a strong friendship, invited her to exhibit her work with the Impressionists. Cassatt, the only American ever officially involved with the group, showed work in four of their exhibitions. Though she was never Degas' pupil, his use of pastels inspired Cassatt and her style developed spontaneity as her technique evolved. Degas is said to have commented on Cassatt's later work, "I am not willing to admit that a woman can draw that well."*

*As she moved away from Impressionism, Cassatt's work throughout the 1880s and 1890s began to focus more and more on the social and private lives of women and the bond between mother and child. In 1891 she exhibited a series of highly original drypoint and aquatint prints inspired by the Japanese masters. She also became a role model for young American artists.*

*Cassatt stopped painting in 1904, after her eyesight failed. That same year she received the Legion of Honor from the French government. Despite her inability to continue painting and drawing, Cassatt advised art collectors, including Louisine and Henry Havemeyer, and remained active in the women's suffrage movement. In 1915 she helped to organize the "Suffrage Loan Exhibition of Old Masters and Works by Edgar Degas and Mary Cassatt" to benefit the cause of the women's movement. Works by Cassatt are part of the permanent collections of both the Philadelphia Museum of Art and the Pennsylvania Academy of the Fine Arts. Mary Cassatt died in France in 1926.*

— Rachel Mamola

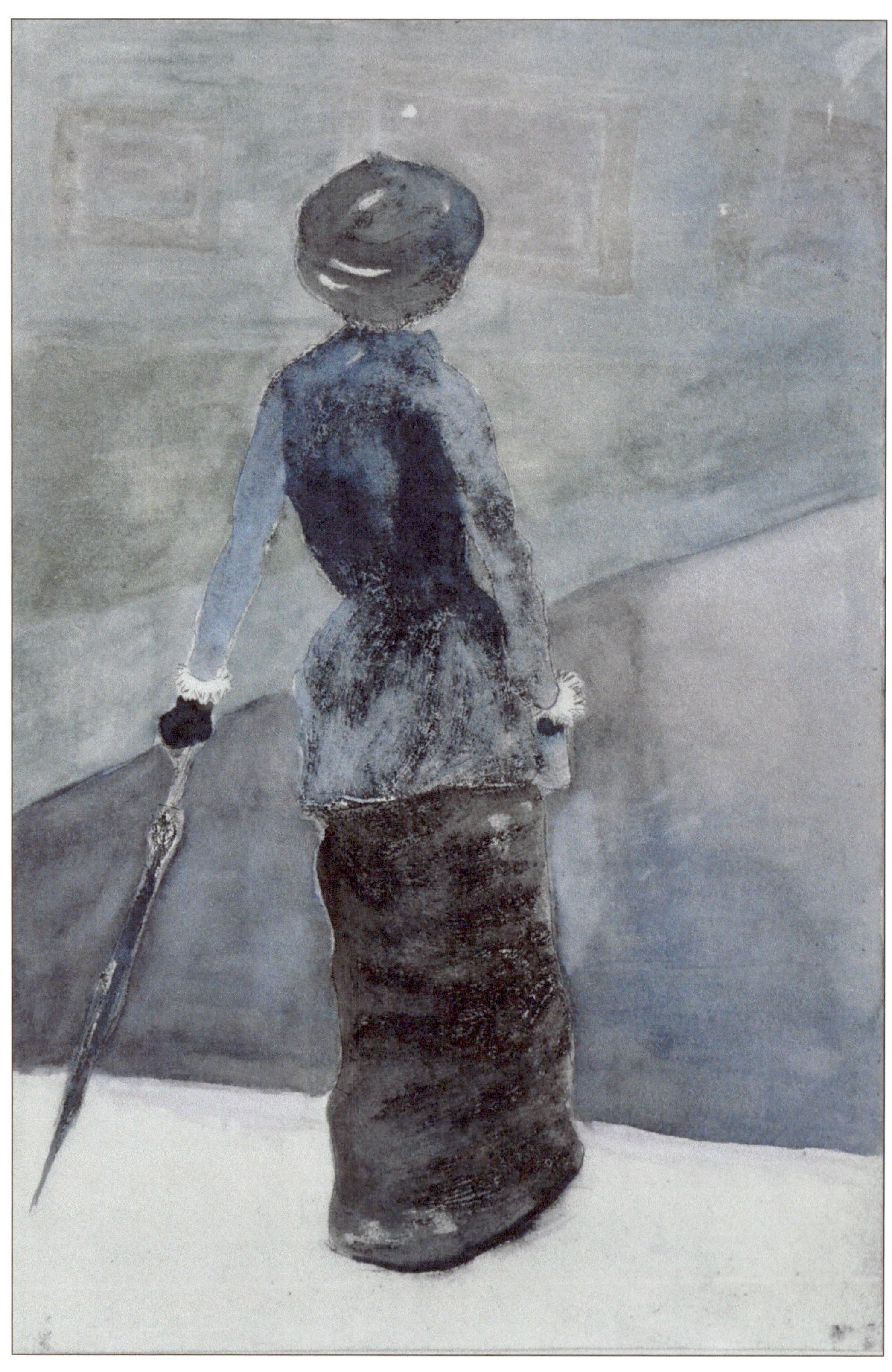

Julia Rix
*Cassatt,* intaglio print with watercolor, 12" x 9"

# THE MAP: 1890

Liz Abrams-Morley

*(after a drypoint on brown laid paper, by Mary Cassatt)*

It is a map of nowhere, no road nor road sign, neither
mountain nor sea. They could be heading

anywhere, two girls, sisters I think, head pressed to head, arm
outstretched, reaching into their imagined futures—all this

Cassatt etched without detail, without her usual plethora
of rose pinks, goldenrod yellows, poppy reds or purples

regal and soft as the irises that bloomed beside my mother's
over-tended rock garden each late spring of my youth.

*You can have it all,* my mother would say as she spaded poor soil,
pulled weeds and paced our tiny yard, the 1950s, exurbia, with the vigor

of a caged cheetah until, late in her life, she thumbed a ride up College,
turned left at Feminism, marched herself out. *You can have children,*

*travel, career, it all—and should,* she meant, *and all at once—*
because she believed that unlike us, she'd had no option.       1968:

*Times have changed,* she claimed, *get up, get out, don't be just a mother.*
This way our maps pointed us, my sister and me,

everywhere, a clutter of highways and lanes, exhaustion days
and weeks of detours, a bridge out, a mountain impassable.

What never changes is time itself: 24 hours in a day, even in Mary C's day,
her hours spent in Philadelphia, in Paris, in concentration, at an easel, leaning over

a copper plate as she rendered the lives men neither lived nor noticed:
baby at breast or on a lap, mother's attention rapt, undivided,

or women sharing tea and secrets, or a woman alone,
brushing out her hair, bathing as her mind floated—where was anyone's guess—

*There's only one thing in life for a woman,* Cassatt once said, *it's to be*
*a mother. A woman artist must be capable of making sacrifices,* but was that road

blocked to her or one that she never wanted to cross? Degas told her:
*Some women paint as though they are trimming hats. Not you.*

*I can live alone and I love to work,* she said.
She said *sacrifices,* but then too: *I am independent!*

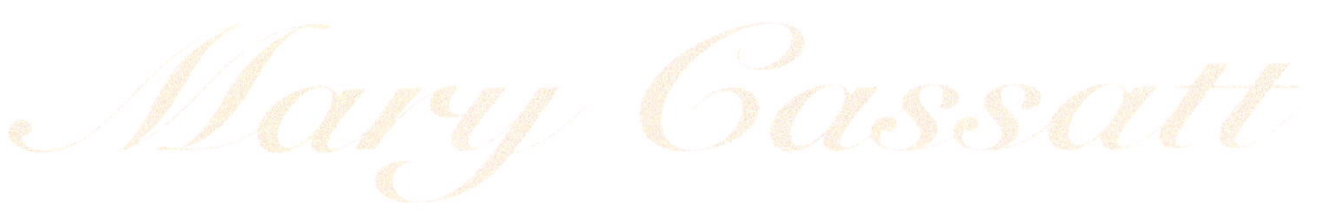

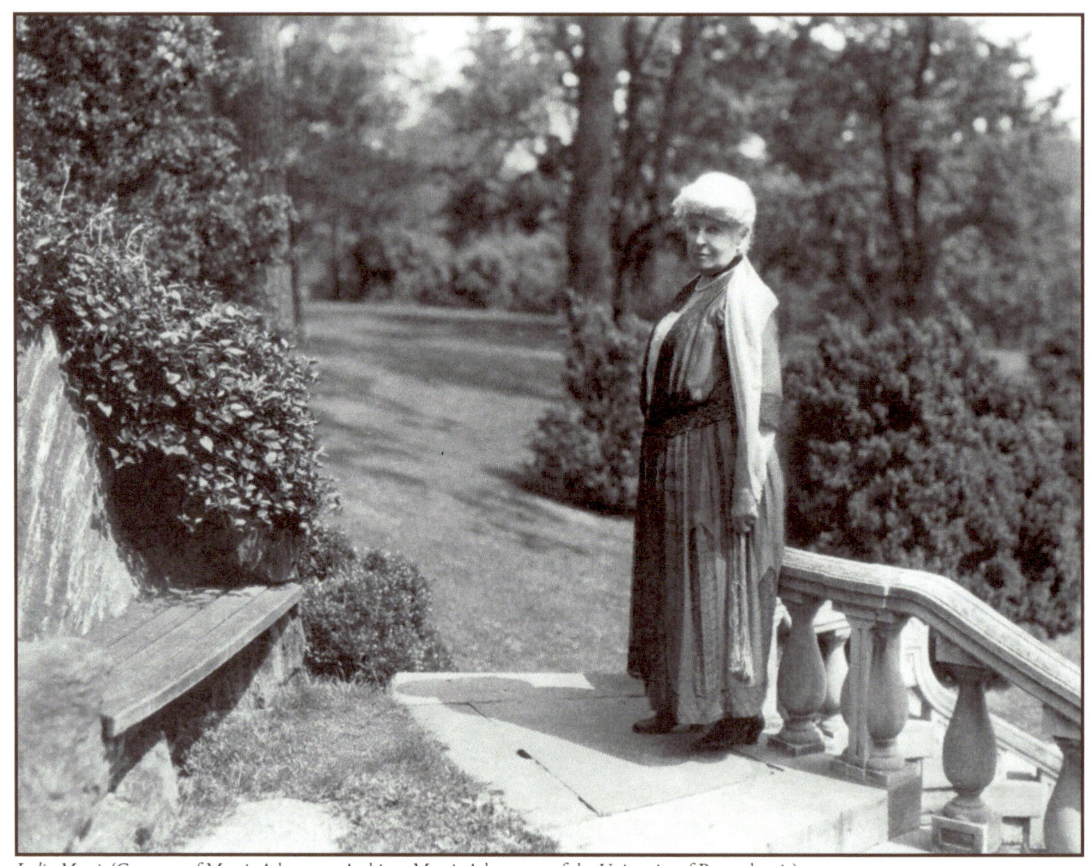
*Lydia Morris* (Courtesy of Morris Arboretum Archives, Morris Arboretum of the University of Pennsylvania)

*"The progress of the world is so rapid and the hurry of life so great that we are apt not to stop and consider the interest which old landmarks may have for future generations ... little remains in our city to show the difference between the past and the present and to mark the changes that take place even in a single lifetime."*

*~from the will of John Morris*

(1849-1932)

# Lydia Morris

*Horticulturist*

*Lydia Morris was an educated, active, and forward-thinking woman whose passion for horticulture and vision for land stewardship and preservation lives on in the beautiful gardens and vibrant educational and research programs at Morris Arboretum in Chestnut Hill. Lydia Morris and her brother John were born to a prominent Philadelphia Quaker family. Their father, Isaac P. Morris, owned a foundry at 16th and Chestnut Streets and made his fortune in iron and steel manufacture.*

*Neither Morris nor her brother, two years her senior, ever married. When John retired and sold the family business in 1881, the pair travelled the world—from England, France, and Italy to Asia, Russia, and Norway—but their many adventures always brought them back home to Philadelphia. The urban sprawl of the Industrial Revolution had left its marks on their childhood home in Frankford and, eager to preserve a legacy for future generations, in 1887 they purchased 26 acres of farmland in Chestnut Hill overlooking the Wissahickon Valley. Here they built their estate, "Compton," which comprised a mansion, carriage house, various outbuildings, and extensive and eclectic gardens. The brother and sister worked with a large gardening staff to tend and develop the property that, by 1913, encompassed more than 166 acres.*

*Lydia shared her extraordinary gifts in the gardens she nurtured, in her active role in civic affairs and encouraging education, and even in the kitchen, where she compiled a handwritten cookbook of her recipes over three decades beginning in 1883. On a trip abroad in 1889, a fellow passenger aboard the S. S. Lahn composed a poem celebrating her sparkling eyes and wit and her brother, "dignified and grave, yet gay… With tenderness fraternal, loving, true."*

*In the course of their extensive world travels the brother and sister amassed a wide-ranging collection of art and craft objects, as well as rare and unusual specimens of plants and trees. They added these treasures to their home and gardens, which they planned would someday be a public garden and educational institution. The philanthropic pair also gifted many pieces of art to the Philadelphia Museum of Art and the University of Pennsylvania Museum.*

*After her brother's death in 1915, Morris continued to oversee the cultivation of the gardens and, at her death in 1932, the property was left in trust to the University of Pennsylvania. Though it might be lost on those of us today who enjoy the freedoms and opportunities that women (and men) of previous generations gained for us, the wording of John Morris's will reflects the strong influence of his sister. His wish was that the property would become "a place where young men and possibly women may be taught practical gardening and horticulture."*

*The gates of the Morris Arboretum opened to visitors in 1933. While the mansion was dismantled in 1968, a rustic log cabin built in 1908 as Morris's private retreat has been restored. Its porch waits for visitors to sit and enjoy, as she did, the stream and woodlands.*

— Tara S. Smith

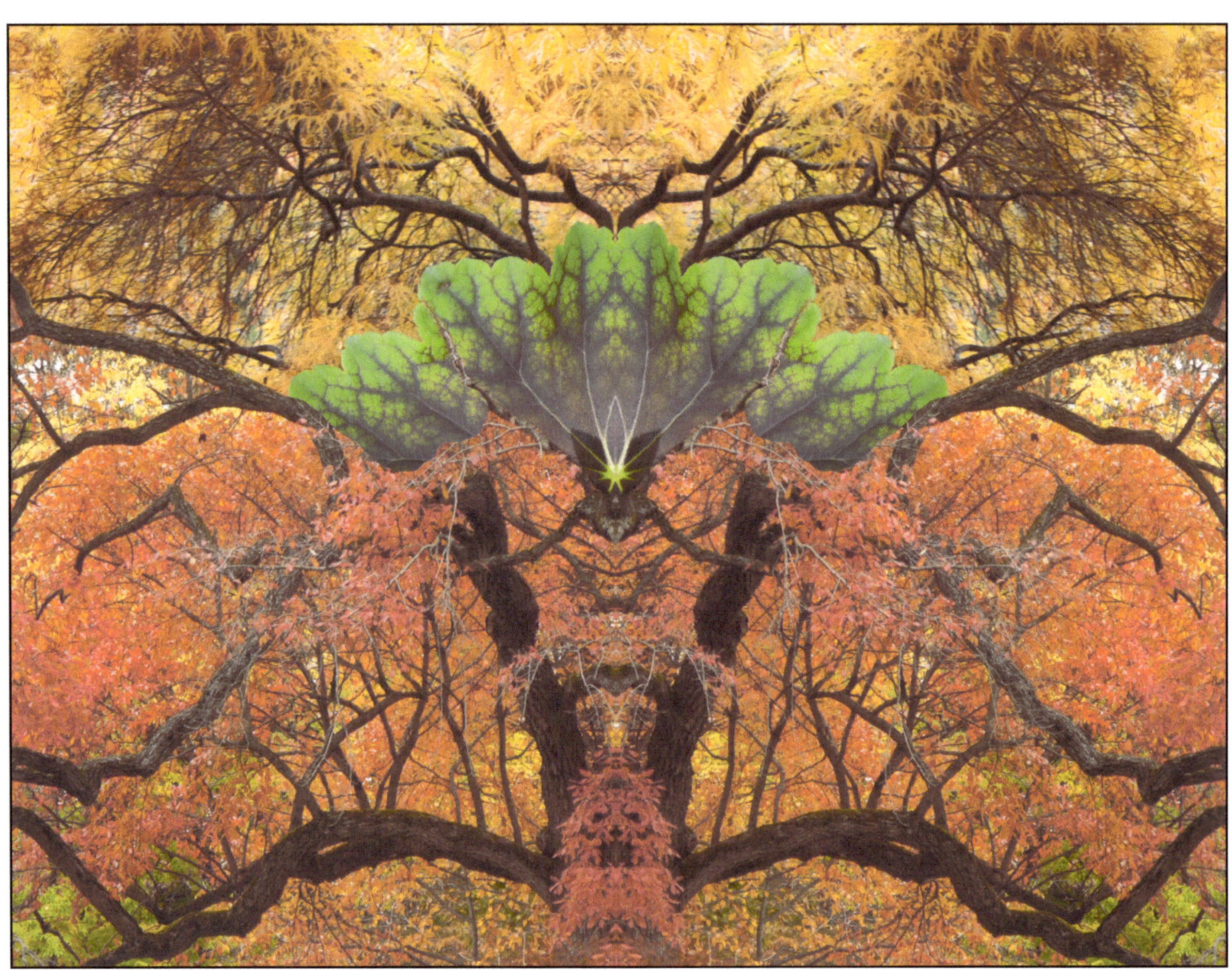

**Suzanne Comer**
*Grandeur,* photomontage, 11" x 14"

Lydia Morris

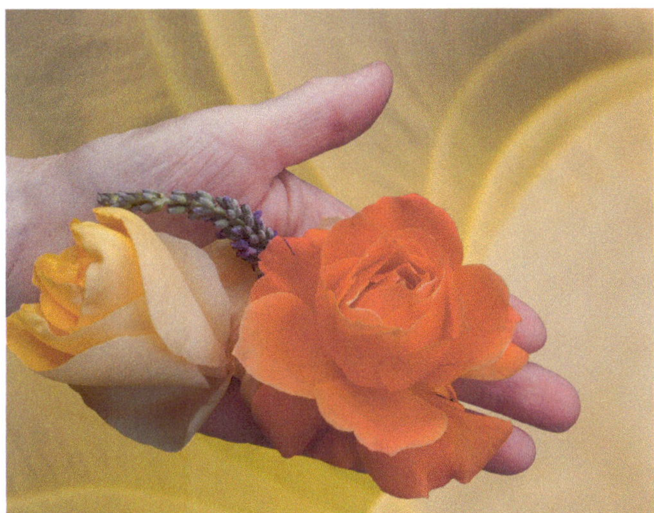

*Gift*, photomontage, 11" x 14"

# COMPTON MANOR

Christine Chiosi

*With her brother, Lydia Morris built "Compton Manor," a summer home, in 1887–88. With remarkable vision, Lydia surrounded it with a horticultural sanctuary now known as Morris Arboretum. The home was demolished in 1968.*

When you listen to sky, brushing
its topaz lips against your ears,
you'll detect my subtle laughter.
Still, some men insist I was razed—
my bedrooms suffocated by maples;
bulkhead trampled by tumbleroot;
stones sunk under swamp magnolias.

I've learned to bear that ignorance.
Discovered joy in befriending soil.
My white chalk mortar bleeding
into mulch's nooks and crannies.
Traveling, entering rosebushes—
suckling roots—as mother's milk.

Have you ever noticed me there?
Turning to velvet blood, climbing
through each plant's thorny veins?
Budding into multilayered blooms?
While damask drapes, having fled
through parlor mullions, create homes
in curled leaves of rhododendrons.

Even hornets' nests, once hanging
from eaves, persevere—buzzing!
As if they never plunged to earth.
Never turned diaphanous. Instead,
sang, bewitching the hazel bushes.

Friends, at night my porch appears.
As does Lydia, overlooking conifers.
Is she an apparition? Or are we?
Figure standing against sapphire
canvas. Eyes glinting. Mouth ajar.
Can you sense her musk perfume?
The tenacity of her hair combs?

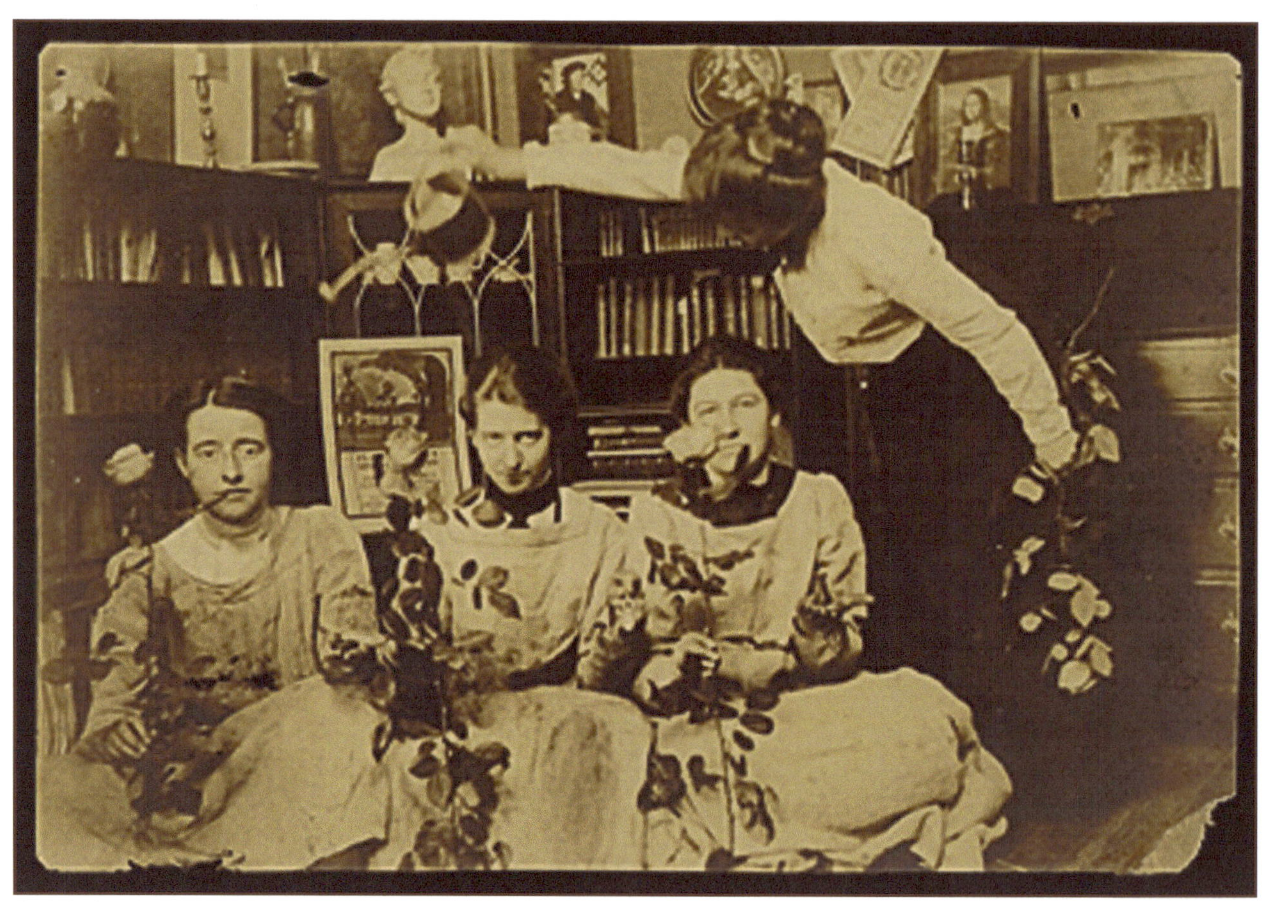

*Elizabeth Shippen Green, Violet Oakley, Jessie Willcox Smith, and Henrietta Cozens (watering the other Red Rose Girls),* ca. 1901 (Smithsonian Archives of American Art)

*"What I want is a desert isle
with a few people I could select."*

*~ Jessie Willcox Smith*

*"... thankful for the blessings sent
Of simple tastes and minds content."*

*~Elizabeth Shippen Green*

*"We three are going out to
where the green trees grow,
where the cows roam and
where the air is pure, and
quietness prevails."*

*~Violet Oakley*

(ca. 1900)

# The Red Rose Girls

*Illustrators: Jessie Willcox Smith (1863–1935), Elizabeth Shippen Green (1871–1954), and Violet Oakley (1874–1961), all accomplished illustrators, were three of the first American women artists to achieve such success.*

*Women at the end of the nineteenth century were rarely encouraged to pursue serious careers in the visual arts. Socially affluent women might take art classes, but never for professional development. And most art schools prohibited women from painting nude portraits. Fortunately, the Red Rose Girls all attended the Pennsylvania Academy of Fine Arts and also studied illustration with the legendary Howard Pyle through a class offered at the then Drexel Institute. Pyle, unlike many of his peers, encouraged his female students to pursue serious careers as artists.*

*Ironically, in order to succeed as professionals, the three women rejected domestic lives of the sort that Smith and Green portrayed so romantically in their illustrations and that later served as archetypes for idealized mother and child relationships. The three artists lived together at the Red Rose Inn in Villanova and later at a home in Mount Airy they named "Cogslea." There a fourth woman, Henrietta Cozens, joined them and encouraged and supported their artistic endeavors by keeping house for them. As contemporary writer and illustrator Alice Carter has noted,*

> *In her 1929 essay* A Room of One's Own, *Virginia Woolf speculated on why so few women have created great literature. She concluded that women could achieve eminence if given educational opportunities, financial independence, and privacy. Had Woolf known about these three American illustrators, she might have revised her formula to include the opportunity to collaborate. For it was certainly their unorthodox lifestyle that relieved Smith, Green, and Oakley of the isolation and domestic responsibilities that still inhibit many capable artists.*[1]

*Jessie Willcox Smith, who also attended the School of Design for Women founded by Sarah Worthington Peter* *(see p. 16)**, is perhaps best known for her covers for* Good Housekeeping *and illustrations for Charles Kingsley's* The Water Babies. *Elizabeth Shippen Green's work appeared in many magazines before she signed an exclusive contract with* Harper's Magazine *in 1901. She was also a prolific book illustrator. Violet Oakley* *(see p. 36)* *is best remembered for her murals.*

*The Red Rose Girls' work became fashionable towards the end of the Victorian era and at the beginning of the modern era and the women's movement, at which point illustration began to be an acceptable vehicle for female artists. Because society viewed illustration as an extension of women's natural talents for decoration and motherhood, many illustrations by other female artists began to appear in children's books and women's magazines.*

— Nicole Contosta

[1] *Alice Carter, "The Cogs of Red Rose Inn,"* Print 51, *no. 1 (1997): 42.*

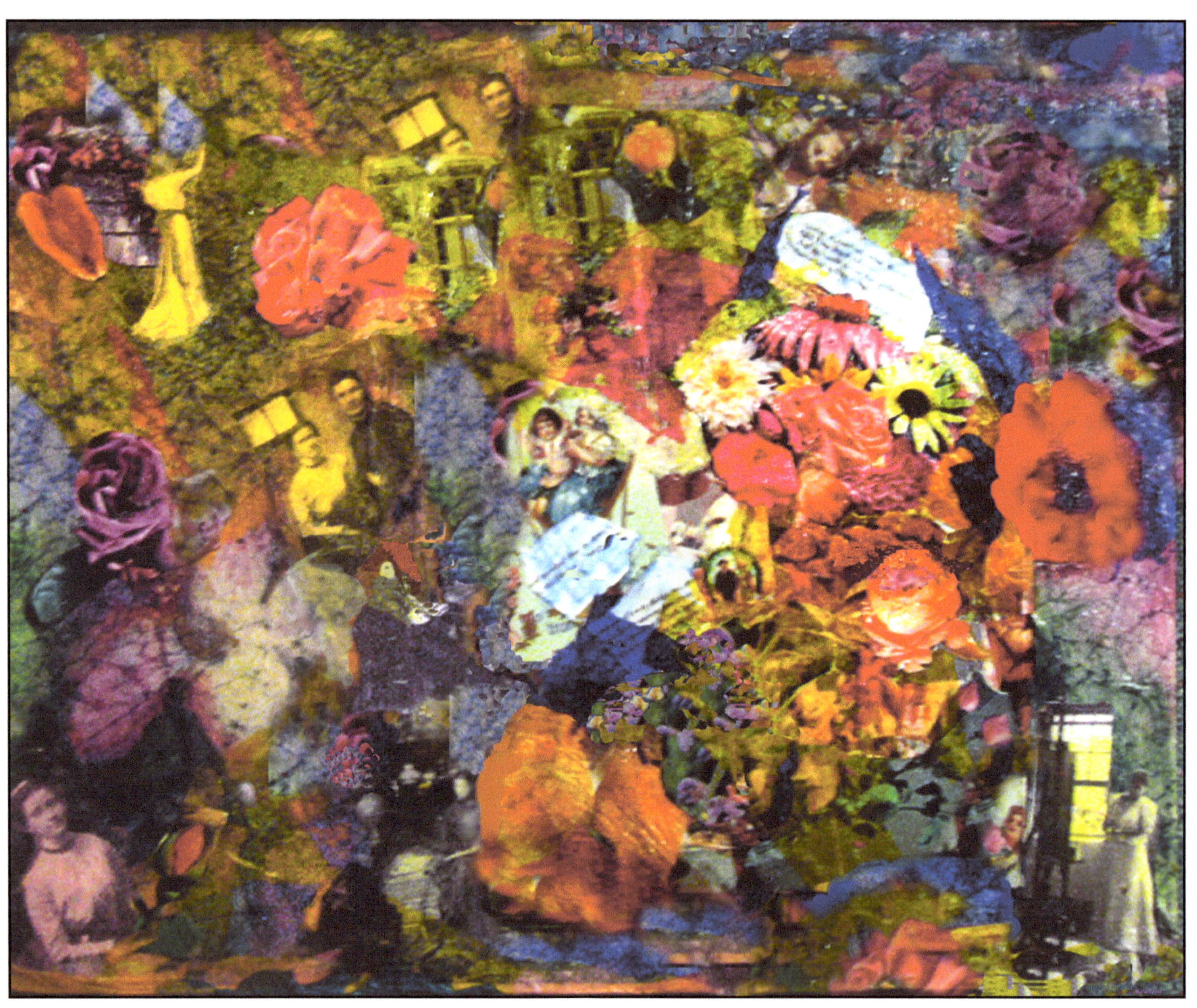

**Maria Keane**
*Honoring the Red Rose Girls,* digital mixed media, 24" x 27"

# RED ROSE GIRLS

Nathalie F. Anderson

*Artists, early students of Howard Pyle, who lived together (with their friend Henrietta Cozens) first at a would-be artists' community, the Red Rose Inn in Villanova, and later in Mount Airy, vowing to stay together their whole lives—though Green married at age forty and left the ménage. Each achieved acclaim—Smith and Green as illustrators, Oakley as a muralist for the Pennsylvania state capitol building.*

## Jessie Willcox Smith

Born, she'd say, in the month of clematis,
nothing morbid or bitter could ever flower
from her paint-brush, but only young creatures
in groping wonder at their strange world: this child,
all hat and belled-out dress, standing on her own white hem
as she thinks to garden; that child toasting serge-socked toes,
burnt orange at the orange parlor fire. Who did not like them—
children—much herself, finding rather in intimate friends
her slush, her hot radiance, she herself so gracefully
awkward. And yet: the cradled baby wide-eyed in the wind.

## Elizabeth Shippen Green

From the age of eight, not *doodling* but *illustrating*
her school notebooks, she got her whole education, she'd say,
lounging that one summer on the Bryn Mawr college lawn,
breathing in the knowledge the college girls left unabsorbed.
Girl on horseback, Girl on sailboat: she saw those students
in their long skirts learning to be sturdy, saw grown women
potting, pruning, stitching, thinking, researching, but painted them
with such elegance you'd say they merely sailed from pose
to graceful pose, the folds of each massive skirt not so much weight
as wing. Yet marriage? *How can she love anyone more than she loves us?*

## Violet Oakley

If ever deprived of paint, she'd say, she could sketch
using only her tongue on the roof of her mouth. Painting
in tongues: she saw herself as Penn's one true disciple,
saw it as her calling to elevate all to civic righteousness,
saw Penn tipping to her his hat, saw Unity—that massy sister—
as his keystone, though was herself not always brotherly
or sisterly—intolerant, insistent, inhuman, spendthrift
with friendship as with cash, volcanic, opaque
even to herself, that small child inside, and yet:
it's just four sonnets, she'd say, from the house to the meadow.

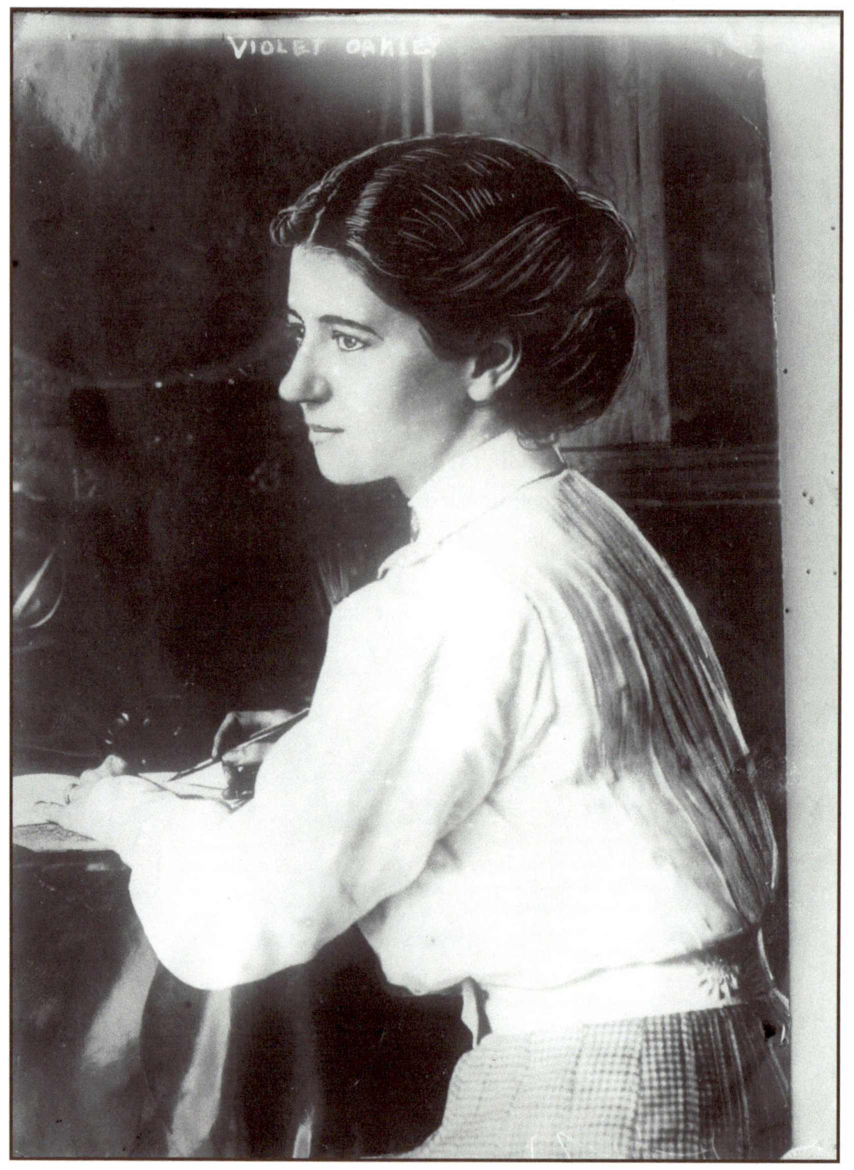


*Violet Oakley,* ca. 1900

*"I must have been a monk in some earlier state of existence … The abbesses and sisters were too busy nursing the sick and doing fine needleworks. I never heard of them illuminating manuscripts. I am quite sure I was a monk."*

*~ Violet Oakley*

(1874-1961)

# Violet Oakley

*Muralist*

*Violet Oakley was born in Bergen Heights, New Jersey and first pursued her passion for painting at the Art Students League in New York. From there she travelled to Paris to study, and then to England. Although she enrolled at the Pennsylvania Academy of the Fine Arts in 1896, her decision a year later—to study illustration with Howard Pyle at Drexel Institute—would shape the rest of her life and career.*

*Pyle introduced Oakley to Jessie Willcox Smith and Elizabeth Shippen Green, and the three women illustrators became known as the Red Rose Girls (see p. 32). Their collaboration, as well as their shared household and vow to remain unmarried and childless, provided them freedom to pursue their artistic careers.*

*Pyle encouraged Oakley to bring her sense of color and design to larger-scale compositions, and she received her first commission—for stained glass windows at All Angels' Church in New York City—in 1899. The New York Times noted that "Miss Oakley ... has steered very cleverly between realism and too much conventionalism, giving her work the stamp of individuality."[1] She counted Pyle and the Pre-Raphaelites among her strongest influences. Oakley's 1902 commission to paint 18 murals for the Governor's Reception Room in the new Pennsylvania State Capitol was the largest ever awarded to an American woman. Her study of William Penn in preparation for painting these murals, which are based on the founding of the colony of Pennsylvania, significantly shaped her thinking and beliefs. From 1911 to 1927, Oakley worked to complete 25 more murals in Harrisburg—in the Senate Chamber and the Court of Law. She travelled to Geneva to document the birth of the League of Nations and published all of these drawings in a 1933 publication,* The Law Triumphant. *Her extensive magazine illustration credits include* The Century Magazine, Collier's Weekly, Harper's, Ladies' Home Journal, *and* McClure's.

*Oakley received many awards for her work, and in 1948 she received an honorary Doctorate of Laws Degree from Drexel Institute. In 1996, she was elected to the Society of Illustrators Hall of Fame. She was a pacifist and part of the women's suffrage movement and was also active in the larger cultural life of Philadelphia throughout her lifetime.*

— Tara S. Smith

[1] The New York Times, *"Mosaics for All Angels': Chancel Decorations Designed by Miss Violet Oakley for the Church on West End Avenue" (Dec. 31, 1901).*

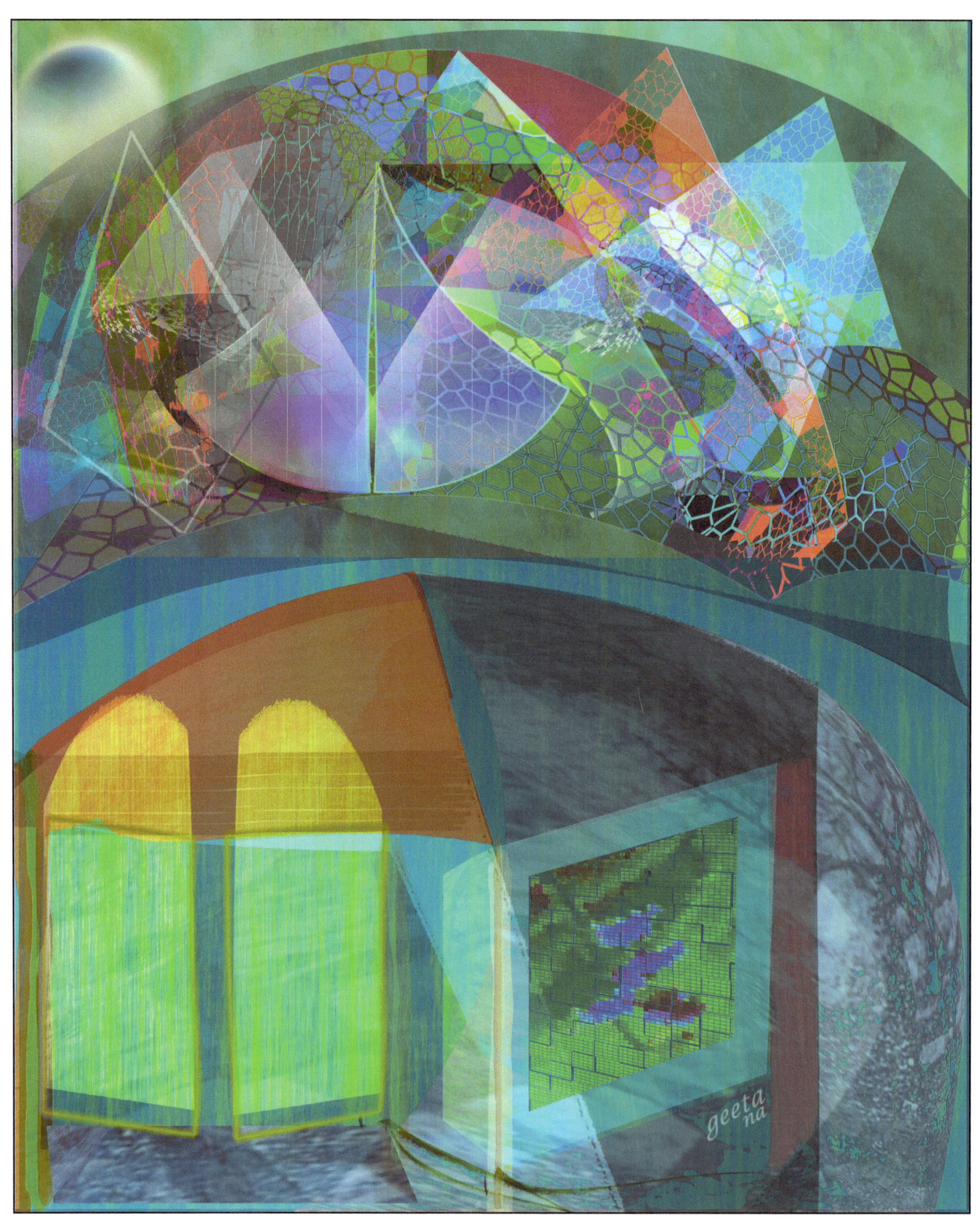


Geeta N. Ahya
*Peace and World Harmony*, digital art, 14" x 11"

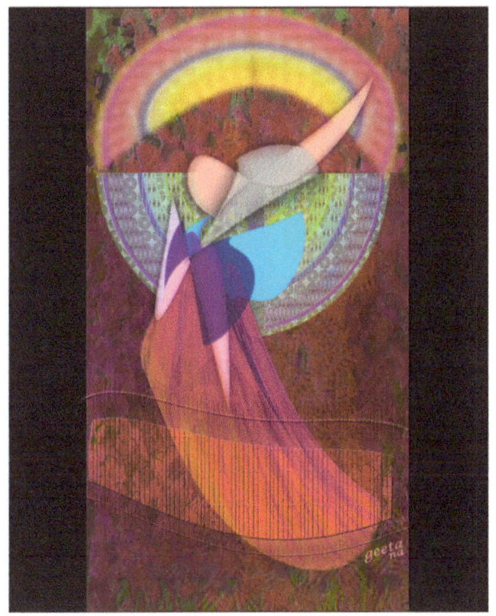
*The Muralist*, digital art, 14" x 11"

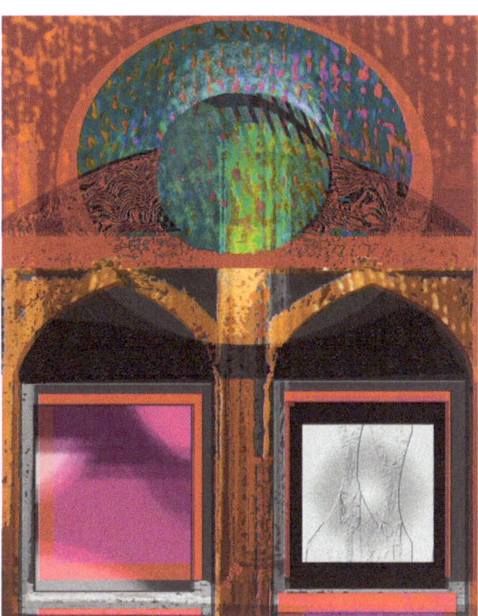
*The Tree House*, digital art, 14" x 11"

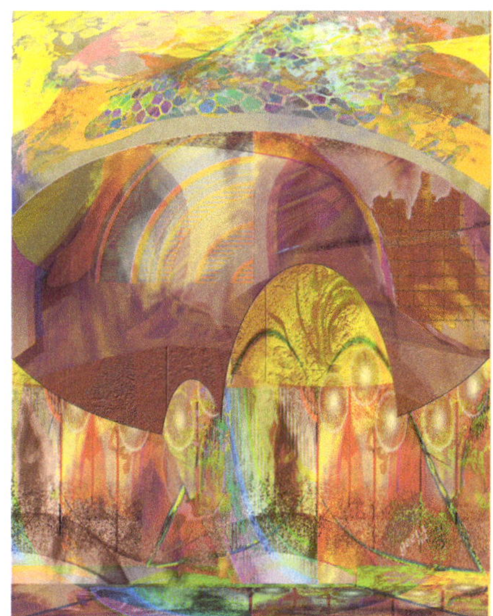
*Illumination*, digital art, 14" x 11"

# NOTE TO VIOLET

Laura L. Buenzle

*Violet Oakley*

Making murals is a lonely art.
In those quiet hours, studio-bound
Could you hear your sisters' laughter?
Did you long to sit within their rooms
And could you smell the garden roses?

I see you drawing on a perch
Focused only on canvas and palette
Forging figures—
Solemn in glance, steadfast in belief
The colors hovering about you

Had such visions not emerged
In strength of line and form
I think they would have split your soul
And silenced you for good

Now your murals hang within our halls
Your spirit pressing in our spaces.

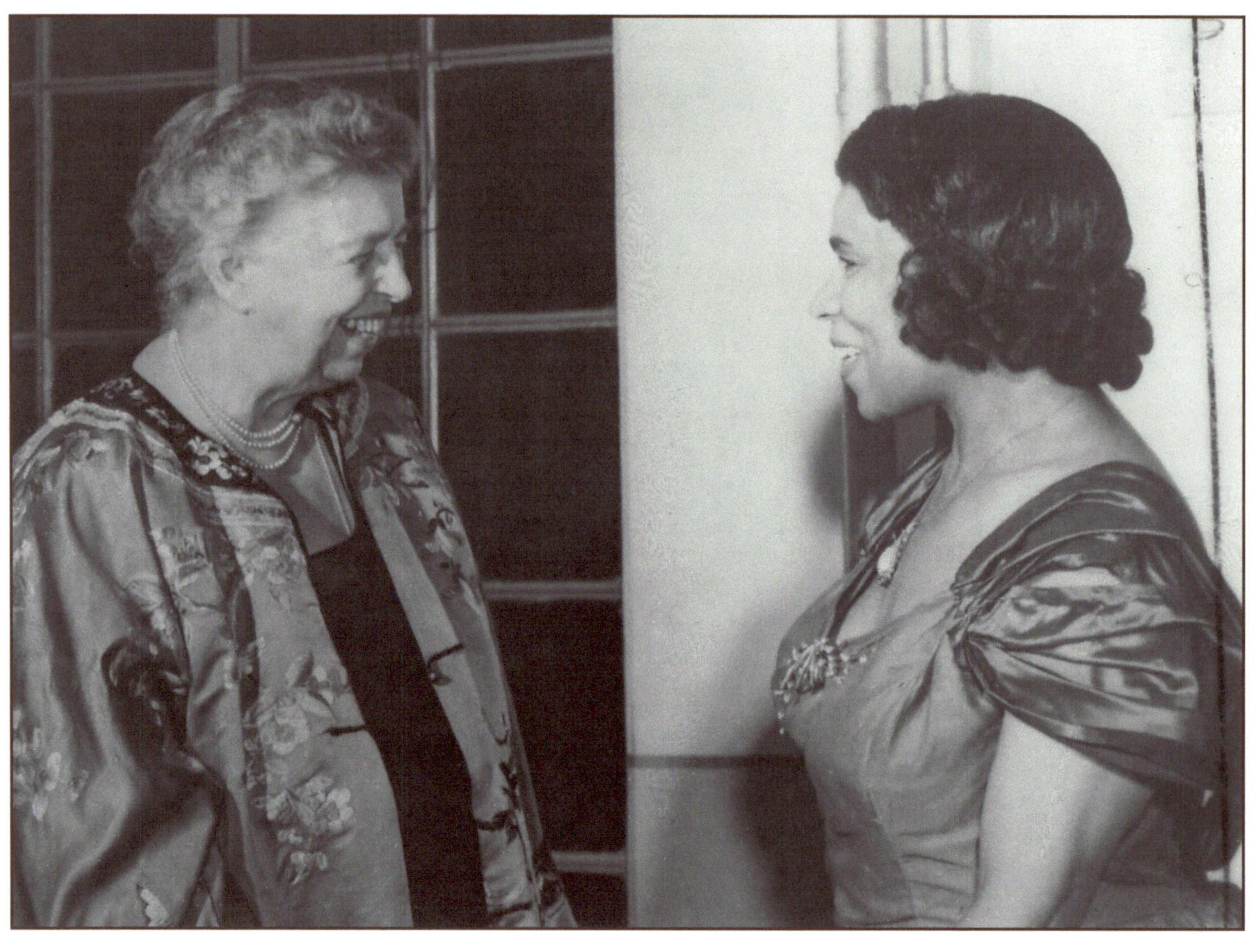

*Eleanor Roosevelt and Marian Anderson in Japan,* 22 May 1953

*"When I sing I don't want them to see that my face is black. I don't want them to see that my face is white. I want them to see my soul. And that is colorless."*

*~ Marian Anderson*

(1897-1993)

# Marian Anderson

*Opera Singer*

*Marian Anderson, the first African American to perform at the Metropolitan Opera, possessed a powerful contralto voice. Her career spanned the globe and nearly six decades. She was born in South Philadelphia in 1897 and joined the choir at her church, Union Baptist, at age six. Her fame as "the baby contralto" spread, and by the time she was thirteen she was receiving invitations to sing at other churches. She taught herself to play piano and violin and transferred to South Philadelphia High School, where she took voice lessons with soprano Mary Saunders Patterson and contralto Agnes Reifsnyder.*

*After graduation, Anderson began to study with Giuseppe Boghetti, who became her longtime teacher and trusted friend. Anderson experienced a setback in 1924 after being criticized for her performance at New York City Hall and considered changing her career path. Her first-place finish at the Philadelphia Philharmonic Society singing contest and her performance at the Lewisohn Stadium competition with the Philadelphia Philharmonic Orchestra the following year restored her confidence.*

*Anderson's success skyrocketed. She began touring in 1926 and received rave reviews for her 1928 Carnegie Hall performance. She went on to tour Europe and Latin America in the early 1930s and continued to receive critical acclaim. Anderson attracted the attention of Sol Hurok, an impresario with whom she signed a contract for more performances in the United States.*

*Anderson's rising success did not come without hardship. Her first audiences in this country were predominantly African American and in 1939, when Hurok attempted to book a concert at Constitution Hall in Washington, DC, the hall manager refused to let a negro perform. His action caused a public outrage. The Daughters of the American Revolution owned the hall, and in response First Lady Eleanor Roosevelt resigned from the DAR and arranged for a concert at the Lincoln Memorial, where Anderson sang in front of an audience of 75,000. In 1943 Anderson performed at Constitution Hall and requested that the audience not be segregated. By the 1950s, she refused to perform in segregated venues.*

*Anderson performed at prestigious venues around the world, including the New York Metropolitan Opera in 1955. She sang at the inaugurations of Presidents Dwight Eisenhower and John F. Kennedy. She was also appointed to the United Nations Human Rights Committee and was awarded many honors, including the Springarn Medal in 1939, the American Medal of Freedom in 1963, and the National Medal of Arts in 1986. In 1941, Anderson used the prize money from Philadelphia's Bok Prize to establish the Marian Anderson Award, which supports young artists. Anderson retired with a final concert in Carnegie Hall in 1965 and died in 1993 at the age of 96.*

*Today, Marian Anderson is celebrated as one of the most influential opera singers of her time, as well as a voice for civil rights and a pioneer for African-American performers.*

— Kara Cochran

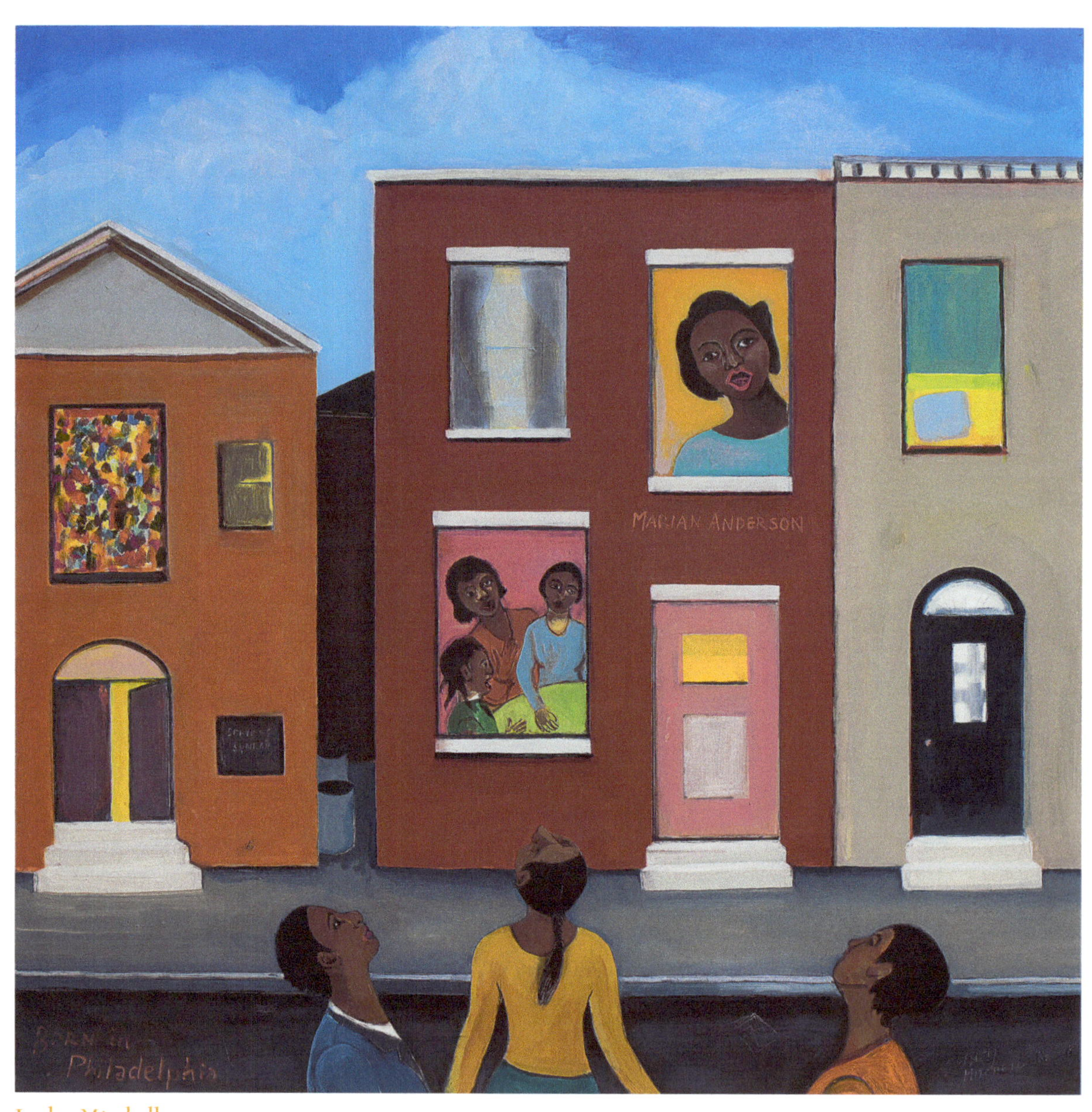


**Lesley Mitchell**
*Marian Anderson of Philadelphia*, oil on panel, 24" x 24"

Marian Anderson

# SWIMMING, SINGING, STANDING

C.J. Spataro

## 1. Swimming

Serita sits on her stoop. A cigarette dangles between her lips as the oppressive South Philadelphia summer heat descends like a woolen mantle. There is no breeze. The block is dark, save the salt glow of the streetlights. A few sweaty kids shuffle down Catharine Street and nod their heads. Serita waves and takes a drag. A few doors down, the new neighbors are listening to opera. The music is soft. The neighbors are friendly and respectful, but Serita doesn't think that she likes opera. Sounds like a cat getting strangled, but it's better than rap, she thinks, all loud and yelling and in your face. Bitch this, and bitch that. She shakes her head. Why doesn't anyone listen to Bill Withers anymore? After she stubs out her cigarette, she looks across the street at the rec center. She knows the center is named after some famous black woman, but she can't remember who, or why she's famous. She gazes at the iridescent surface of the pool, shimmering in the moonlight, and rakes her sticky bangs back up over her forehead. What would she give to be in that pool, to feel the cool caress of the water? Sometimes, during the day, she watches the swimmers from her upper floor window and imagines putting on a bathing suit, slipping on some flip-flops and flouncing over there, but she never goes. One of these days, she thinks, she's going to walk across the street and take the plunge.

## 2. Singing

Your parents have a weird record collection. You don't understand the collection, or your parents. Neither your mother or father seem to like music much. But here it is: Ramsey Lewis, Sergio Mendes, Blood, Sweat, and Tears, Stokowski, and the Philadelphia Orchestra performing "A Night on Bald Mountain," Caruso. Your mother constantly tells you to turn the music down, as if it is an audible expression of her unhappiness. You settle on Marian Anderson, *Spirituals*. You're working on some spirituals for your college recital. You've been listening to Leontyne Price, mostly. You love her because she's not perfect. Your voice teacher looks at you thinking: here we go, another crazy white girl singing "Deep River." "Fuck Deep River," you tell him. You want to sing "Ride on King Jesus!" not because you're any kind of believer, but because the music is, well, everything you're not. When you're singing you can be someone else, someone with a different set of problems, someone with a different life. You find the track and drop the needle. No one is home, so you crank it up and sing as loud as you want. This version is not the same arrangement, but close enough. Your mother comes home in the middle of the opening chorus and drops her bag of groceries on the kitchen table. You're singing fortissimo: "No man can a hinder me!" You stare at her, daring her to stop you. She walks to the stereo and turns the music off. "Go unload the car for me," she says.

## 3. Standing

February 26, 1939.

My dear Mrs. Henry M. Robert: Jr.

I am afraid that I have never been a very useful member of the Daughters of the American Revolution, so I know it will make very little difference to you whether I resign, or whether I continue to be a member of your organization.

However, I am in complete disagreement with the attitude taken in refusing Constitution Hall to a great artist. You have set an example which seems to me unfortunate, and I feel obliged to send in to you my resignation. You had an opportunity to lead in an enlightened way and it seems to me that your organization has failed.

I realize that many people will not agree with me, but feeling as I do this seems to me the only proper procedure to follow.

Very sincerely yours,

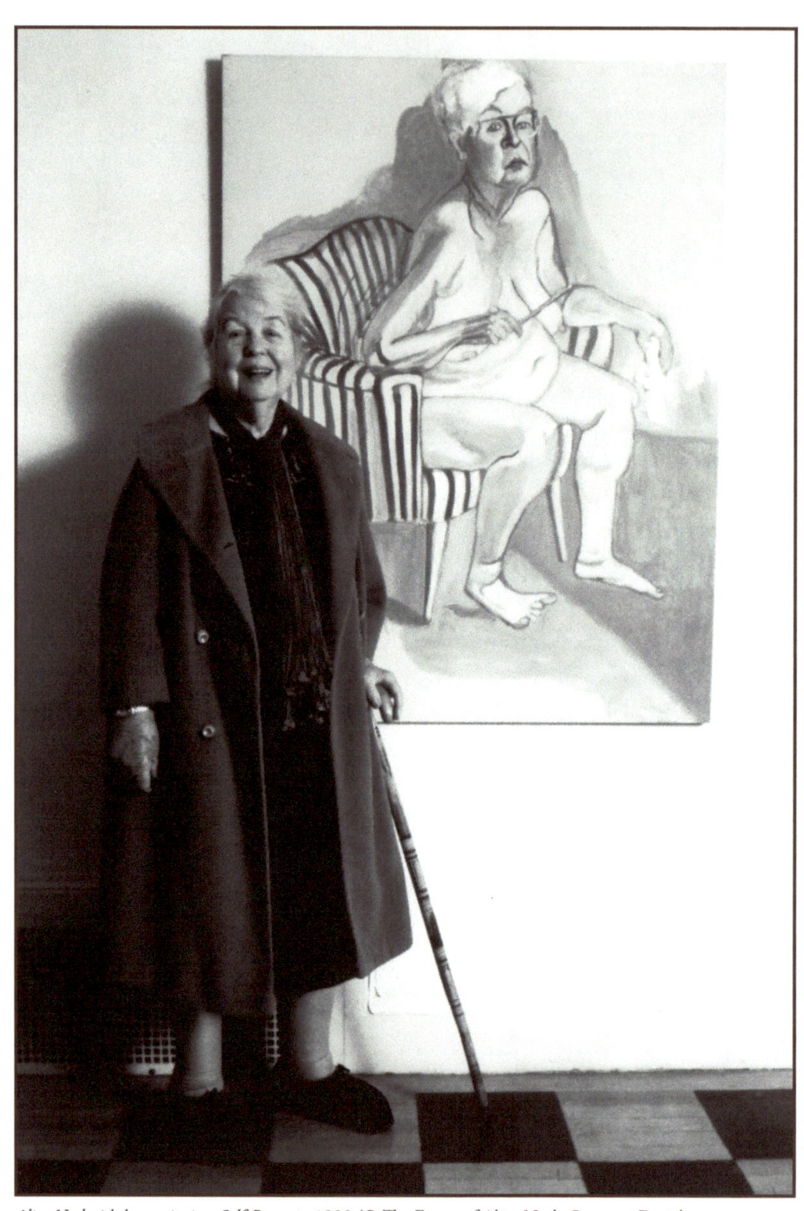

*Alice Neel* with her painting *Self-Portrait*, 1980 (© The Estate of Alice Neel, Courtesy David Zwirner, New York/London)

*"All experience is great providing you live through it. If it kills you, you've gone too far."*

*~ Alice Neel*

(1900-1984)

# Alice Neel

*Portrait Painter*

*Many remember Alice Neel as the artist who painted Andy Warhol in the swinging 1960s. But Neel, who moved to Greenwich Village in 1927, was an original bohemian. Neel spent her time pursuing a non-traditional life with the Village's non-conformists, poets, and artists. Neel hailed from the affluent Philadelphia suburbs. She was born in Merion Square and, like Jessie Willcox Smith (see p. 32), studied at the School of Design for Women founded by Sarah Worthington Peter (see p. 16). After graduating, Neel lived in Havana for a year before settling in the Village (then Harlem).*

*Neel suffered personal upheavals, including the death of her infant daughter, that colored her work and informed her themes of loss and human vulnerability. In 1930, she spent time in the suicide ward of Philadelphia General Hospital. A year later, Neel recaptured that experience in a pencil on paper portrait.*

*Unlike that of many artists, Neel's style did not change with the times. Throughout her career, Neel painted candid, intimate portraits. Critics see the expressionism of artists like Vincent Van Gogh, Edvard Munch, and Diego Rivera as influences in Neel's work. Neel continued to paint in this style even after it went out of vogue in the post-World War II era.*

*Although Neel lived in relative obscurity until the 1960s, she was able to earn a living with her art. During the Depression, Neel worked for the Works Progress Administration capturing scenes chronicling the lives of striking workers, impoverished families, and the homeless.*

*Many credit Neel's emergence as a celebrated artist late in life with changes in society. Some attribute this to the women's movement of the 1960s while others note the art world's return to interest in the human form. Besides Warhol, Neel painted several other large-scale yet inventive portraits of artists, including Frank O'Hara and Faith Ringgold. She even painted her own self-portrait at the age of eighty.*

—Nicole Contosta

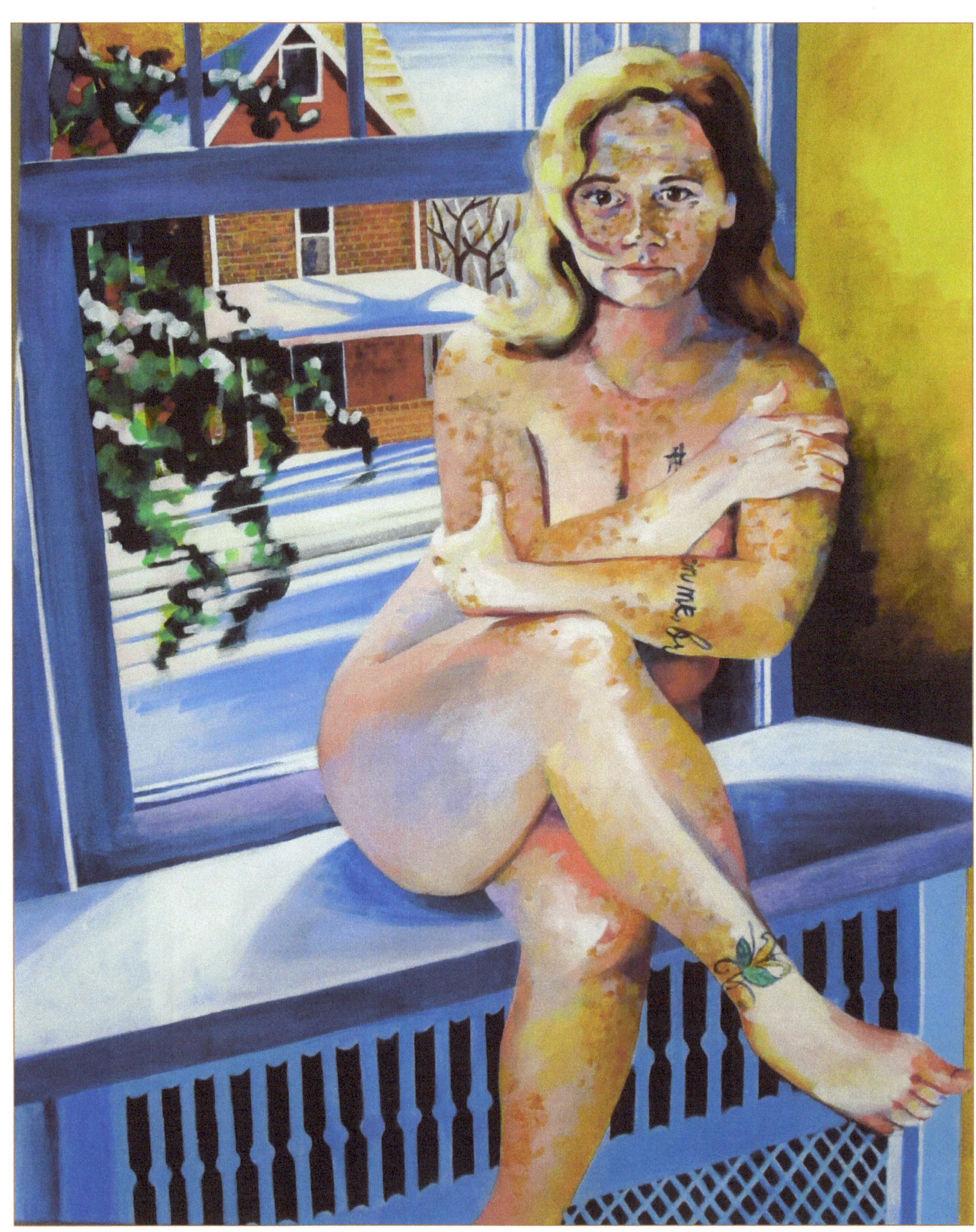

Melissa Tevere
*Baby, It's Cold Outside*, acrylic on canvas, 30" x 24"

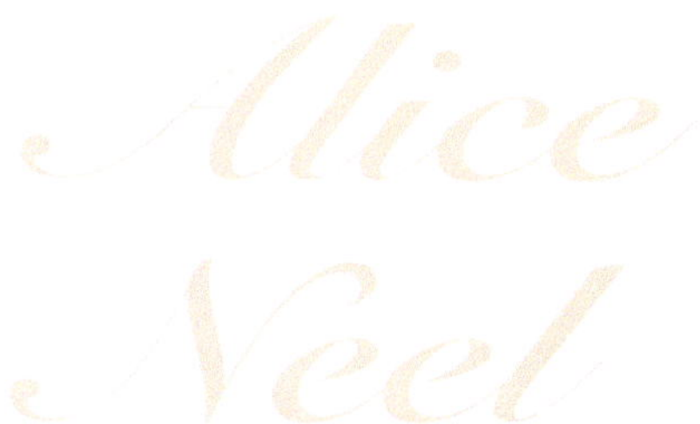


# PRISCILLA JOHNSON

## *Gives in to Another Pipe Dream*

Nicole Contosta

If Tom tells me to smile one more time, I'll scream. And if he tells me to be happy because I'm a pretty girl, that's it, I'll leave. I've already sat here, rigid with resentment, for the last few hours as he tried to rationalize losing my life savings on his follies production. What idiot gives her money to a man she just met?

But he took me to Minsky's old place. He traded jokes like an old vaudevillian for cocktails.

Maybe it was watching him earn money on the spot as a performing artist. Maybe it was the setting. The Winter Garden has a rich history as a former burlesque hall—before Mayor LaGuardia banned it twenty years ago. Besides occasional paint jobs and structural repairs, very little had been done to rehab the venue. Wooden beams supported its high ceilings. It was a cold night in January. The upstairs became so drafty that people huddled under their coats for warmth. What a faded relic.

Then they played the flick. It was the Gershwin's . Sitting in the balcony under the darkened lights, it wasn't a stretch to imagine the show girls, the comedians like Abbott and Costello, decades before. I remembered my mother telling me that it had been a favorite haunt of her brother's after he quit work at the clerk's office in the 1930s. And I'd always romanticized what it must have been like for the performers, traveling from town to town for a series of "one night stands." Those performers had survived on their talent alone. My limbs burned with romantic fervor. I've danced my entire life.

That happened last week. Tom planned to revive the art form through a cross-country tour. I spent my last penny on this shiny green dress. Everything was set to go. But the band leader took off with the investment.

He can talk all he wants. I'm getting away from here.

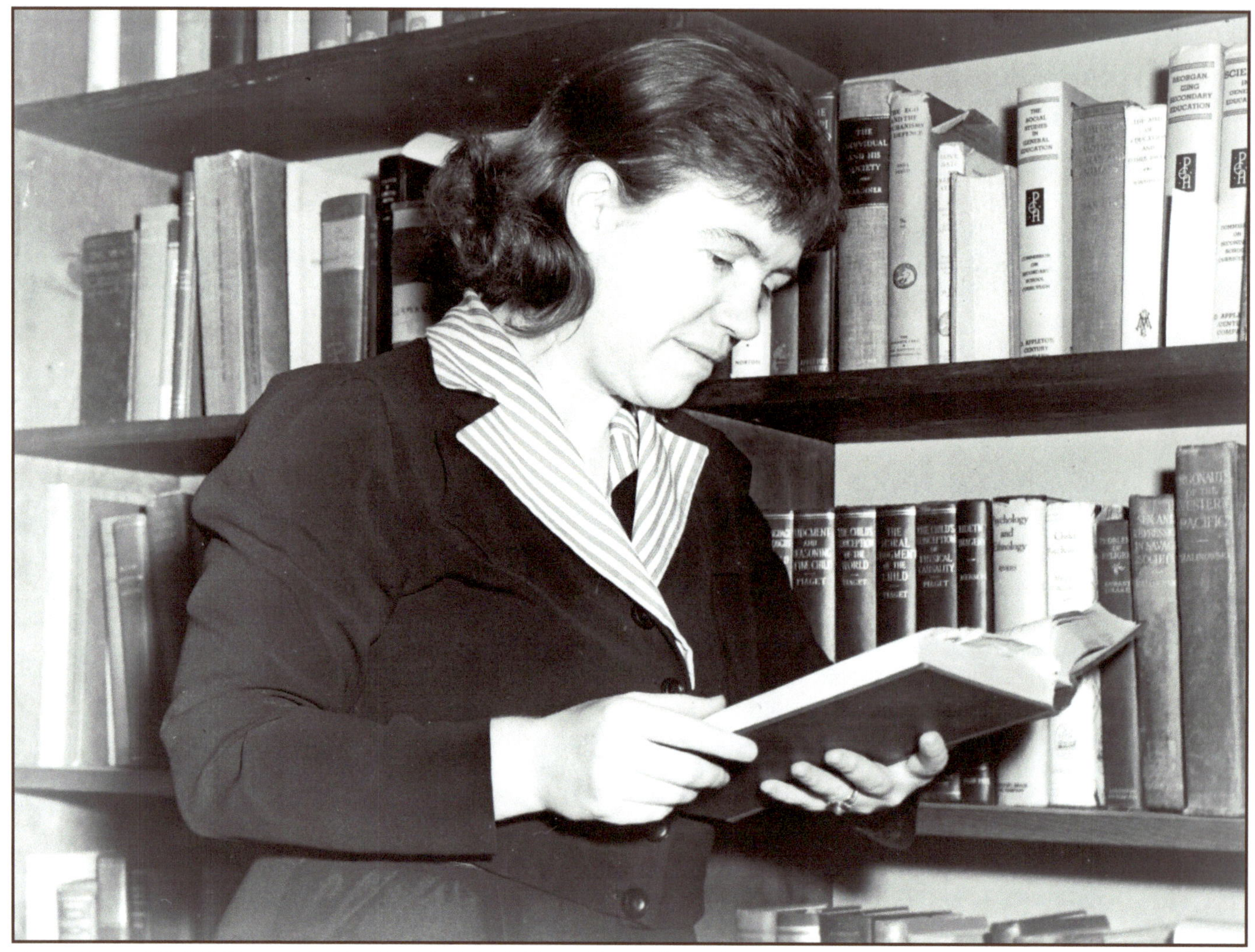

*Margaret Mead*, ca. 1930-1950 (Photograph by Edward Lynch for the *World-Telegram*, Library of Congress)

*"I do not believe in using women in combat, because females are too fierce."*

*~ Margaret Mead*

(1901-1978)

# Margaret Mead

*Anthropologist*

*Margaret Mead was an anthropologist, American icon, writer, intellectual, wife times three, mother times one, deemed "mother to the world" by* Time Magazine,[1] *and founding mother of the feminist movement.*[2] *Not satisfied with simply adding to the academic literature in her field, she popularized her findings, "translating anthropological insights garnered from non-Western societies into meaningful and accessible critiques of American society."*[3]

*Mead was born in Philadelphia, the oldest of four children. Her father was a professor of economics and her mother was a sociologist. As a child, Mead's father had told her it was a "pity that she wasn't a boy," because she could "have gone far."*[4] *Clearly, Mead ignored her father's limited vision for her. She graduated from Barnard College, earned an MA and PhD fromColumbia, and went on to become a household name.*

*Mead studied non-literate cultures of the South Seas and wrote about her findings in 44 books and over a thousand articles.*[5] *She was an innovator both in the topics she chose to study and in her research methods. She used observation to gather data and incorporated photography and film in her work. Extrapolating from her research of other cultures, Mead expanded and transformed how "twentieth-century women and men conceived of themselves… laying the groundwork for today's concepts of gender and sexual identity."*[6]

— Tori Bond

[1] *Paul Shankman,* The Trashing of Margaret Mead: Anatomy of an Anthropological Controversy *(Madison: University of Wisconsin Press, 2009), 3.*

[2] *Nancy C. Lutkehaus,* Margaret Mead: The Making of an American Icon *(Princeton: Princeton University Press, 2008), 72.*

[3] *Ibid., 6.*

[4] *Ibid., 22.*

[5] *"Margaret Mead 1901–1979,"* Anthropology, *University of South Florida, October 26, 2013, http://anthropology.usf.edu/women/mead/margaret_mead.htm.*

[6] *Ibid., 82.*

# Margaret Mead

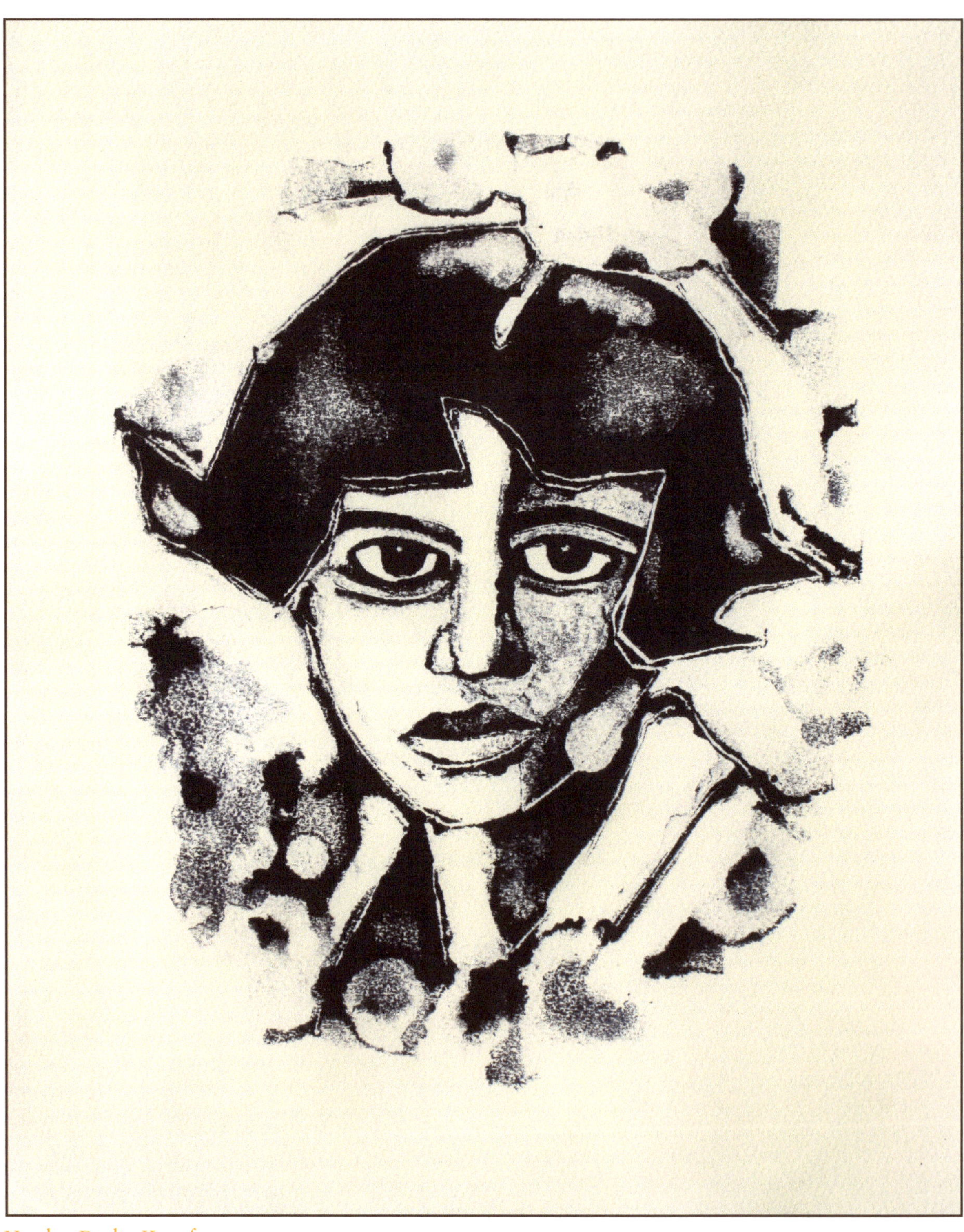

Heather Devlin Knopf
*Young Margaret Mead*, monotype, 14" x 11"

# INVOCATION

Julie Odell

My tender nipples swell and I curl into myself. Other girls at school pull their shirtwaists tight, shoulders thrown back, giddy, but my own body fills me with dread. Soon enough I'll have to marry. I'll spend my days as a hostage in a house filled with children and nights in bed with a man I may or may not love. I'll have nothing of my own, least of all the freedom to open the door and go where I want.

That summer I sit in the window seat in the upper hallway of my father's house and look down on the big leaves of the catalpa tree as they shimmer in the soft wind. If my gaze gets lazy, I can see girls, dusky-skinned, wandering languorously in the shade, their own breasts unfettered and their shoulders relaxed, for this, the awful metamorphosis, is nothing to them.

Their life is not the inevitable march to womanly despair, instead a kind of soup, thick, parts on the surface and other parts obscured. Their passage has no urgency. It's the most delicious time, and they spend it like cats in the sun, waiting for the next pleasure to tumble past so they can reach out and bat it with a paw.

On these long, syrupy days, they can love whomever they want, reach up and drag this boy, that girl down onto the soft grass, and they can lie together, taste each other, kisses and strokes, skin on skin. Then on to the next, and another after that, and no one cares, no one calls them whores or shutters them off to a convent.

When at last all appetites are sated, the girls might make a baby. This man or that—someone to build a roof and bring food and keep them warm at night. It doesn't much matter because everyone belongs to everybody, and this is just most practical with children.

I long to be among them, to burst free of my awful binding underclothes, to let my skin go golden in the sun and my hair fall loose down my back. I see their world so clearly, and I know it exists, somewhere, so when the time is right, I pack my things and leave my father's house, go off to university. The girls from school laugh and say it's a shame I'm too plain to marry so college is my consolation prize. They can say whatever they want—they are now captives, but not I.

I work hard on my studies, and at last the big professors give me my papers. I let them think it's their idea, to send me off to a distant land to do their research, and it's there I find the girls lying in the sun and immerse myself in their world, finally, finally.

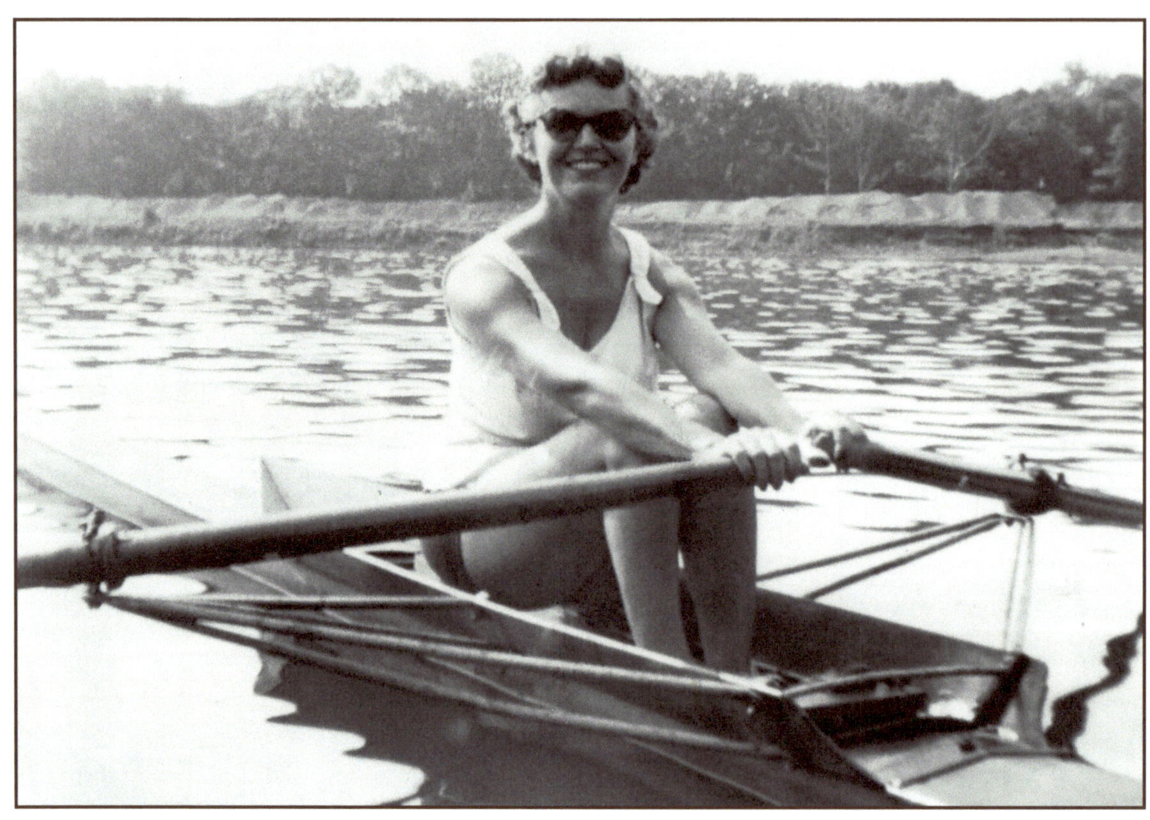

*Ruth Robinhold*, 1938 (PGRC Archives)

*"I loved it that we organized the club. It was to educate young girls with rowing. I never dreamed we'd be in competition. We were the mommas of women's rowing."*

*~ Ruth Robinhold*

# (1913-2012)

# Ruth Robinhold

*Rowing Pioneer*

*Ruth Robinhold helped to organize the Philadelphia Girls' Rowing Club in 1938 so that women could finally take to the Schuylkill. None of the other clubs on Boat House Row at the time allowed "members of the weaker sex" to row. Robinhold, who is remembered for her generous spirit, energy, and laughter, inspired and encouraged generations of women and girls to participate in the sport she loved.*

*Robinhold enjoyed gardening, laughter, and a good martini (which she credits for her longevity). Her famous martini recipe: Add two shots of gin and one shot dry vermouth to a shaker half-full of ice cubes. Serve with a twist of lemon. Key ingredients for her inspiring life include faithful service, loyalty, courage, and a sense of humor.*

*Ruth embraced the challenge of balancing a 1-foot wide by 30-foot long boat with the characteristic verve she brought to all of her long and active life. She met her first husband, William Henry Robinhold, when he offered to help carry her boat in after an outing. He rowed with the Undine Barge Club (next to the PGRC). "I didn't need any help whatsoever," Ruth said as she recounted the tale years later, "and I usually sent all offers packing. But him—well, I liked the look of him and I decided he could carry my boat any time." They were married for 63 years until his death in 2003.*

*While Undine repeatedly offered her an honorary membership in later years, she always refused. "I like my club, thank you very much!" she said. "It's a nice offer, but where were they when we had to fight to get our own club started and no one would lend us equipment or coach us? So no thanks—I'll stick with my girls."*

*Robinhold was born in Germantown and was a long-time resident of Lafayette Hill. During World War II, Robinhold volunteered as a nurse's aid at Hahnemann Hospital after a full day of work at the John B. Stetson Hat Company. After twenty-four years with Stetson, she worked for another twenty as manager of mortgage insurance at the First Pennsylvania Bank. With a degree in horticulture from The Barnes Foundation, she also grew award-winning rhododendrons and worked tirelessly in various gardening clubs and societies.*

*Of her many interests and passions, her "girls" at the PGRC always took first place. "'We were girls in the beginning, and we were Philadelphia girls,' Robinhold said with a laugh. 'Many, many women belong to the men's clubs. We don't want men. We're chauvinist pigs. It's for women educating other women. It's been much of my life.'"*[1]

*Robinhold continued to row on the Schuylkill well into her eighties, and in 2007 she met and married Richard Lewis Henderson. She maintained active membership in the PGRC, whose meeting room is named in her honor, until her death in 2012.*

— Tara S. Smith

[1] *Ira Josephs, "Rowing their own way: Ruth Robinhold secured a place for women on Boathouse Row 65 years ago,"* Philly.com, *June 17, 2003, http://articles.philly.com/2003-06-17/sports/25448270_1_boathouse-row-undine-barge-club-honorary-member.*

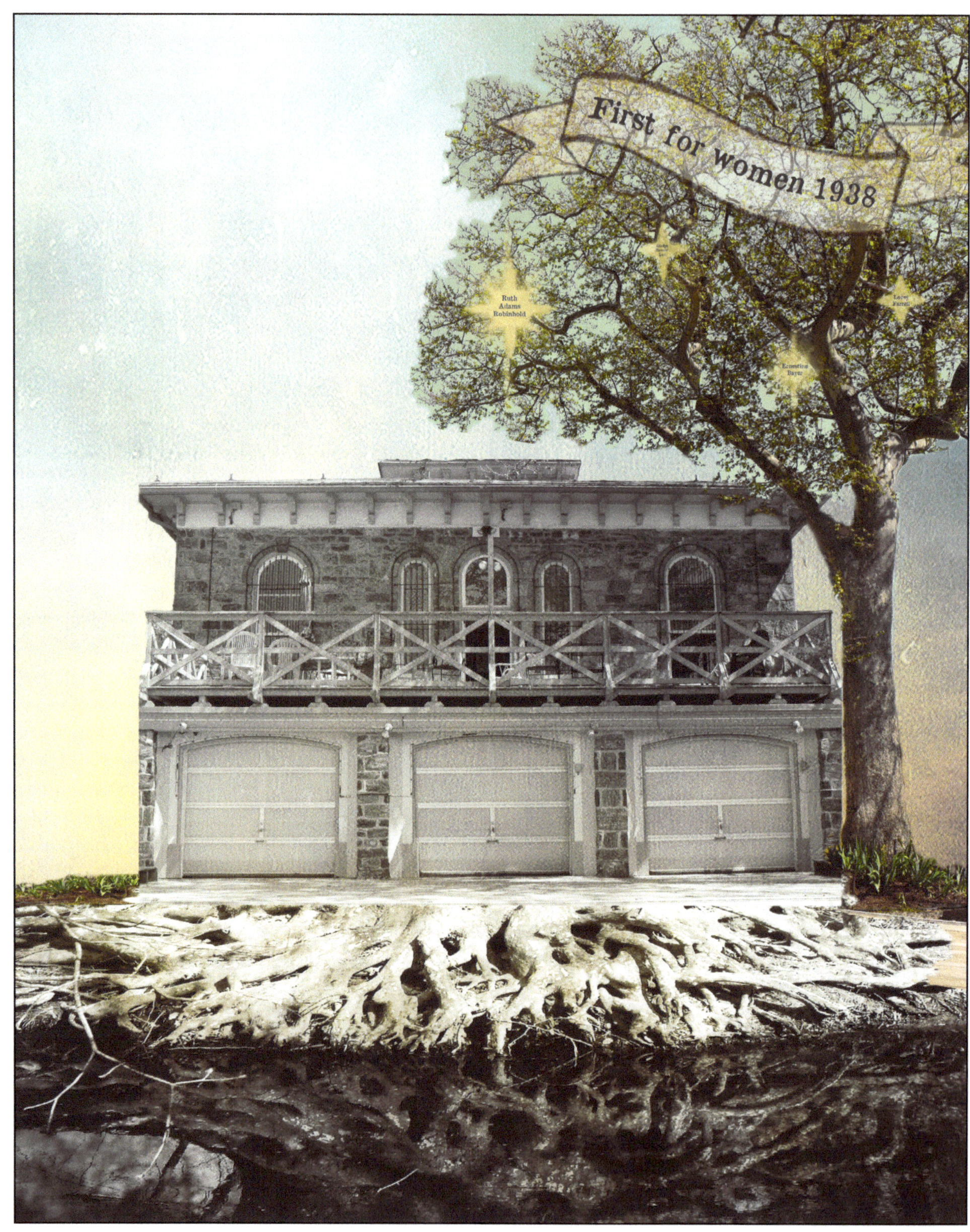


Michelle Ciarlo-Hayes

*First for Women,* photographic collage, 14"x 11"

# WHO WOULD HAVE THOUGHT?

Carol Rabuck

On the occasion of your 90th birthday the men sang "Let Me Call you Sweetheart"
That was always the way.
They revered you, even in the beginning.
"She was quite a looker"

You were 25 in 1938, showing up with 16 others who pooled their efforts, afforded the five dollars each for a rental, then a mortgage at number 14 Boathouse Row
Choosing to be separate rather than beholden.

Only one of you had a car, yet you made your way, followed the commands and pulled your first oars up the Schuylkill:
"Hands on the boat, lift. Walk it out. Up and over heads! Split opposite! Weigh enough! Toe to the edge and in! Count down when ready: Bow, two, three, stroke. Shove off! Ready all? Row!"

The men had helped you—vowed you to secrecy
"Right hand is port and left is starboard, facing backwards to head forwards. Drive the legs and hold them down. Swing from the hips, recover long, reach to catch and drop the blades in, drive again, extract and feather. Relax and glide to feel the run."

At first you go where they tell you to go but then
You make your own way, looking over your shoulder, steering the shell upriver on the same course under tall bridges and trees.

At eighty you rowed a double with a younger member.
Carried the shell (as you insisted) down the dock
Stepped in balanced on one leg then gently seated.
Each of you blended to become the other,
plying strength, experience and water
"She was such a pleasure. Technically correct. Controlled. Phenomenal."

When diatribe of gender may have given way to scorn you might have said,
"What's all the fuss about? Let's row!"

You rarely missed a meeting at your club, the walls now lined with trophies.
Seventy-four years later and going strong, sharing a hearty handshake.
Enjoying celebrations and mixing a mean martini.
"She is someone I would want to be"

And of the women who followed you live on a generation,
Their family names repeated in the racing programs.
World champions, Olympians, reflected in your contributions.

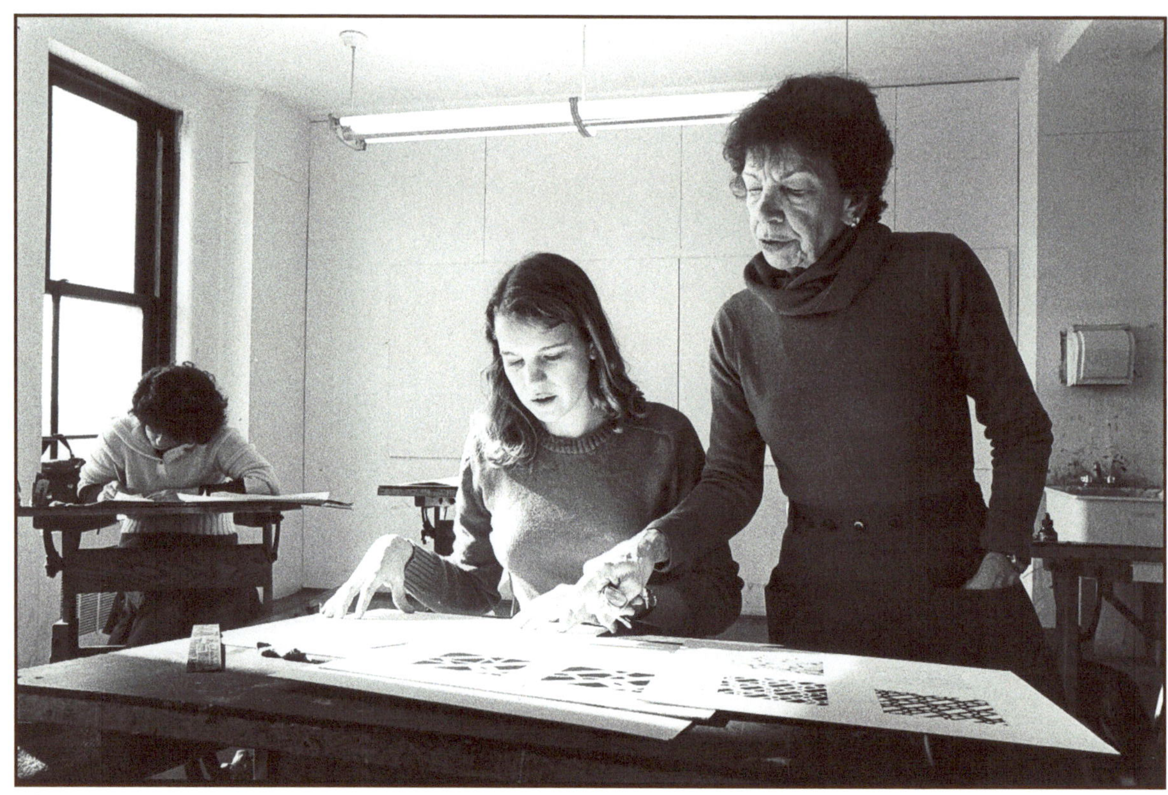

*Edna Andrade,* ca. 1970s (University of the Arts, Philadelphia)

*"I am concerned with geometric systems, ratio, color interaction, visual ambiguities, scale, archetypes. My ideas come from organic structures, crystallography, physics, gestalt psychology and from games, patterns, puzzles and sunsets at the end of Pine Street."*

*~ Edna Andrade*

(1917-2008)

# Edna Andrade

*Op Artist*

*Edna Andrade made a bold impact on the Philadelphia art world and beyond with six decades of work and three decades of teaching at what is now the University of the Arts. She was a Philadelphian with a southern drawl who adopted Philadelphia as her home in 1946. She grew up in Tidewater Virginia, studied at the Pennsylvania Academy of the Fine Arts and at the University of Pennsylvania, and then began her teaching career in the public schools in Norfolk and then at Tulane University. She married Philadelphia architect Preston Andrade in 1941. After doing design work for the government during World War II, she assisted her husband in his architecture firm and also did freelance drafting. One of her freelance projects included plans for the Philadelphia airport. Andrade's divorce in 1960 "allowed her artistic career to flourish."[1]*

*Andrade's body of work began with and returned to realism, but she is most known for her Op Art, which uses contrasting colors and meticulous geometric shapes to create the "hallucinatory"[2] and "undulating"[3] illusion of motion. The influences of science and architecture are evident in much of her work, as she drew inspiration from "everything from astrophysics to Freudian psychology."[4] Andrade describes her Op Art as "form and color—what you see is what you get. There's no story that comes with that."[5]*

*Andrade received the College Art Association's Award for Distinguished Teaching of Art in 1996, and in 1997 the Edna Andrade Emerging Artist Award was established by the Leeway Foundation in her honor. Andrade's art can be viewed at the Philadelphia Museum of Art, the Pennsylvania Academy of the Fine Arts, and many other museums throughout the country.*

— Tori Bond

[1] *Edward J. Sozanski, "Esteemed Phila. Artist Andrade dies,"* The Philadelphia Inquirer, *April 18, 2008.*

[2] *"Edna Andrade Optical Paintings 1960–1966,"* Locks Gallery, *January 12, 2007, http://www.locksgallery.com/exhibits_works.php?eid=43.*

[3] *Amy Rosenberg, "An Outpouring of Art,"* The Philadelphia Inquirer, *September 14, 2012.*

[4] *Ibid.*

[5] *Edna Andrade, as quoted in Julia Rubalevskaya, "Art exhibit gets rave reviews,"* The Daily Pennsylvanian, *January 21, 2003, http://www.thedp.com/.*

# Edna Andrade

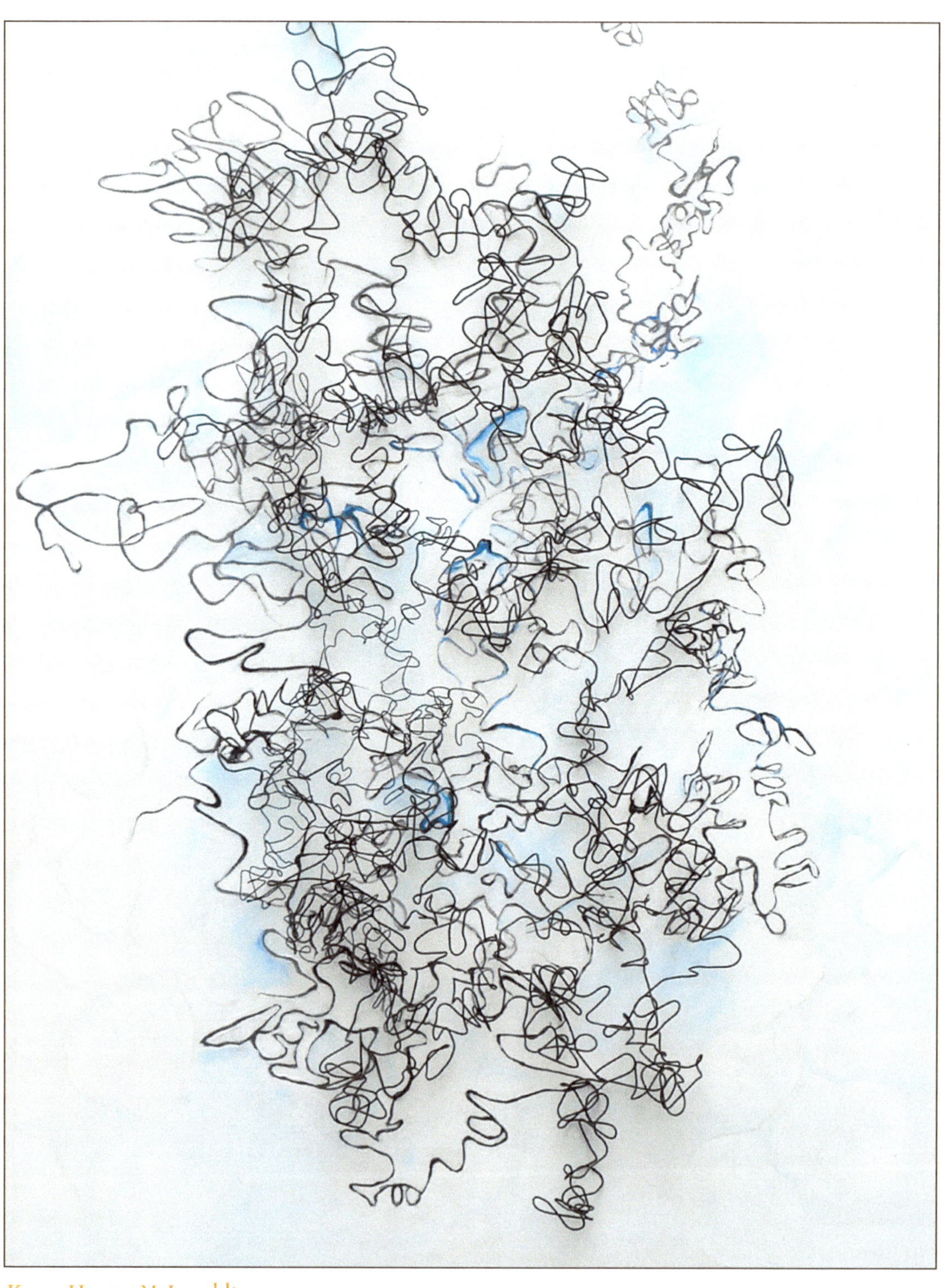

**Karen Hunter McLaughlin**
*A Mind of Her Own Illusion*, mixed media, 48" x 36"

# SYNESTHESIA:
## *Edna Andrade's Op Art Speaks*

Tori Bond

### Turbo 1-65, 1965

Dog gleans much information through his tongue: wet like puddle or toilet, crunchy like stick or bone, salty like sweaty face or gritty toes. Tongue data rarely makes dog stop consuming anything. I have no sense organ as luscious as a tongue with which to lick at the world. I am creative spark but have no function like Wite-Out or Play-doh. I could be wallpaper. I could be jigsaw puzzle. I dream of being a dress. I am precision on linen, lines, and angles. I have an eye but cannot see. I observe you while you observe me. Creator-mother licked me into existence with wet turquoise, wet orange. Look at me! I will spin but cannot move. Stare at me! I will climb into your head, shove the furniture to one side, set your inner compass gyrating, and watch you wobble. Creator-mother does not visit anymore. I miss licking.

### White Dragons, 1968

I am Aegis of Zeus, Medusa head nailed to shield, an impotent protector to a people tearing itself apart, writhing for change. I hiss down narrow passages, spiraling through deep mazes of your mind, exciting the unconscious chaos of your white matter while Zeus releases his sons upon this nation like hounds of war, hunting plunder. Dionysus intoxicates with free love, peace protests, and riots, white against black, while Apollo, god of order, orbits the earth and moon in a rocket-powered chariot. Ares wages war within and without, battling oppression of racism and communism. Stare if you dare. I, unlike the hideous Gorgon, will not repay your curious eyes with stony transmogrification but there is a cost. Greedy gods demand supreme sacrifice for the transformation of a great nation, and the Furies respond, offering up Bobby and Martin. I am a meticulous metered precision, a slithering light against shadow, weaving in and out of your dark grey matter. I offer myself as the absent order, the light in dark times, a counterbalance to Dionysian frenzy of 1968.

### Space Frame Study, 1965

I am collapsing quasar seen through cone-starved eyes of a black Labrador named Sparky, framed by the rearview window of a '65 Chevy Impala. Hungry for knowledge, Sparky licks at the cool glossiness that is the plane upon which he sees the mathematical equation for The Theory of Everything. I am that plane. I am the incomprehensible universe of galactic nuclei folded in on itself like an origami black hole. Sparky's limited tongue knowledge has no translation for numbers or geometry. Some creator beings would consider this a tragedy, that the universe would reveal itself to the one who cannot understand. Sparky is unbothered by his ignorance.

*"In case my paintings are ever 'discovered' after I'm dead, this is my statement of what I was trying to do. I loved the appearance of things, light particularly, and I tried to copy it as accurately as I could, leaving out what was boring and exaggerating what I liked. Why I loved certain sights better than others I never understood, and neither do the people who are explaining it to you now."*

*~ Alice Steer Wilson, inscribed on reverse of "Windsor in September," 1974, from Janice Wilson Stridick,* Alice Steer Wilson: Light, Particularly *(Merchantville, NJ: Southbound Press, 2013), p. 1.*

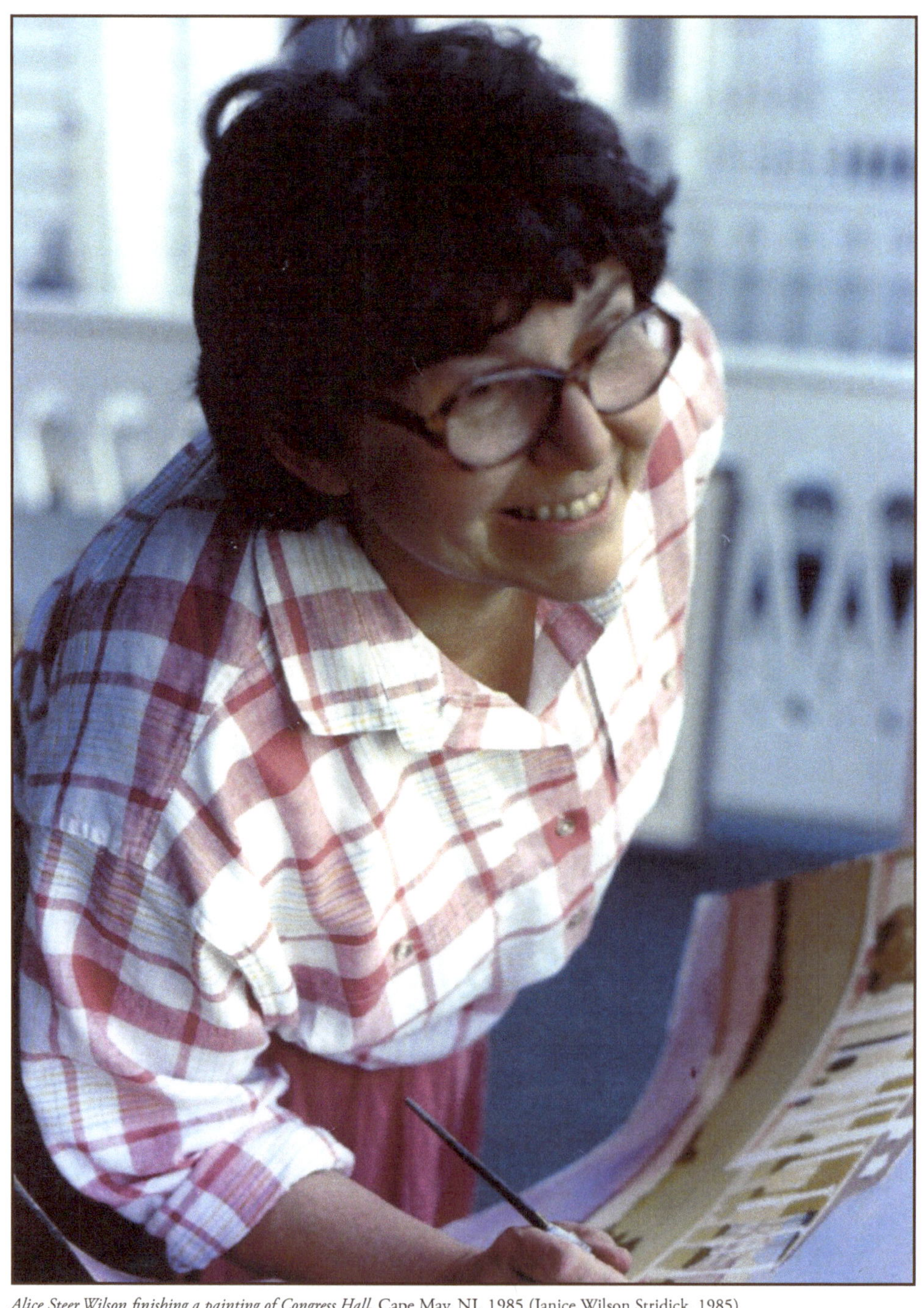

*Alice Steer Wilson finishing a painting of Congress Hall,* Cape May, NJ, 1985 (Janice Wilson Stridick, 1985)

(1926-2001)

## Alice Steer Wilson

*Artist, Teacher*

*Alice Steer Wilson grew up in North Lima, Ohio. Her passion for art began in her youth, during summers on Long Island Sound, and she painted until the very end of her life.*

*Wilson graduated from Oberlin College in 1948 with a degree in psychology. After working with the Haddonfield Arts and Crafts League in the 1960s, she attended the Pennsylvania Academy of the Fine Arts in Philadelphia to study painting, printmaking, and drawing. It was outside the confines of education where Wilson began to flourish as an artist. She studied the old masters and had particular regard for Van Gogh, Vuillard, Cassatt, and Hopper.*

*Wilson lived with her family in Moorestown, NJ, but spent summers in Cape May from 1971 until her death. She fell in love with the Victorian buildings and the way the changing light transformed the landscape and structures. She painted and drew outside on the sidewalks and beaches. Her work grew in popularity when, in 1977, she and her husband Fred printed her watercolor paintings of Cape May onto note cards.*

*While her watercolor paintings are popular for their commercial appeal and she has been occasionally, but affectionately, referred to as "Mrs. Cape May," Wilson was an award-winning, commissioned artist for her oil portraits and she taught painting and drawing at Gwynedd Mercy Academy and Stockton College, among other venues. It is estimated that Wilson completed about two thousand works of art in her lifetime, more than two hundred of which are included in a book compiled by her daughter, Janice Wilson Stridick, titled* Alice Steer Wilson: Light Particularly.

*After Wilson was diagnosed with breast cancer in 1995, she completed over fifty paintings per year during the last six years of her life. Remembered as a visionary artist in a community of preservationists, Wilson's work is collected internationally.*

— Rachel Mamola

# Alice Steer Wilson

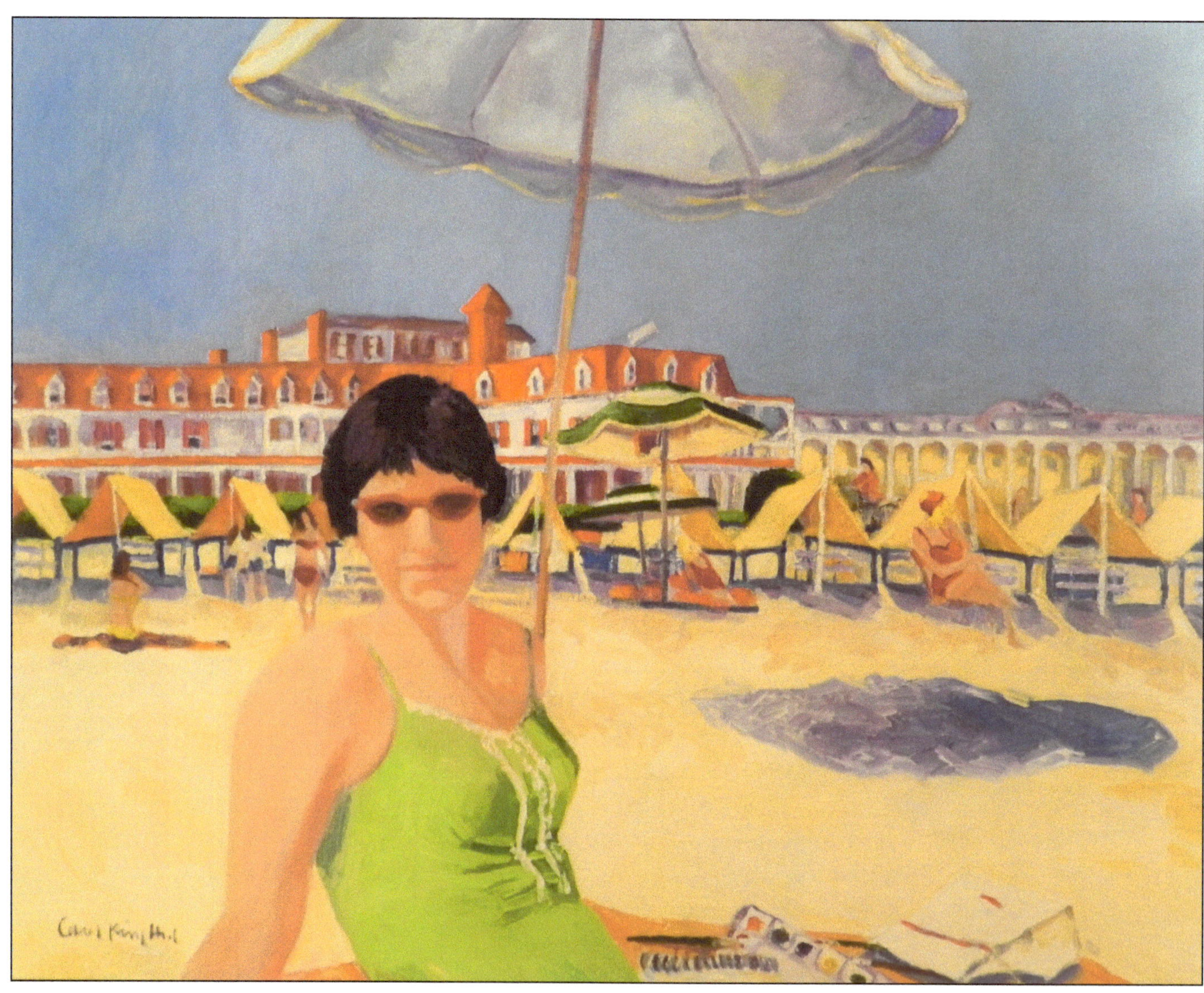

Carol King Hood
*Alice through Rose Colored Glasses, oil, 24" x 36"*

# MOTHER'S SELF-PORTRAIT WITH HAIR

Janice Wilson Stridick

The gaze, mouth firm, sets the Academy straight, while
earth-green watercolors drip down a shock of white.

Never shown, never mentioned, unsigned—
she must have known, left in her bin, I'd find

this undercoated sheet of flesh
and sky. A column of earth and slate

back up a portrait of reprieve, painted
as her straight black hair grew in curly, close.

Freed from chemo and wine, she signed masterpiece
after masterpiece, wrote *OK Forever.*

Red flecks light the mohair on her shoulders—
a shawl I gave her when she lost her hair.

Now, that earth-green wrap is mine:
each time I touch it, I drape myself in art.

Each time I add a painting to her catalog,
her startling, fearless eyes confirm *press save.*

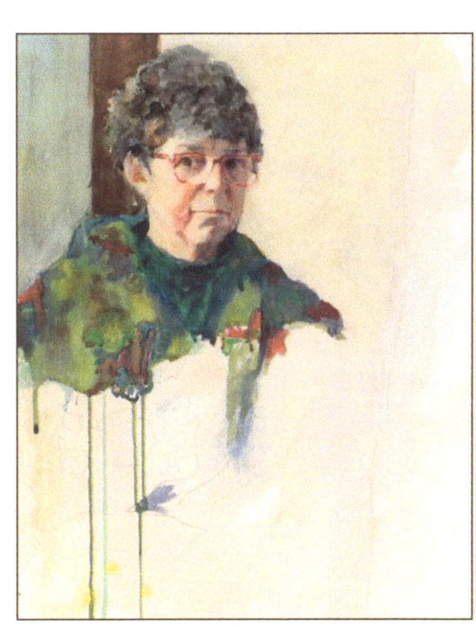

*Watercolor and graphite on paper,*
*22" x 18", 1996*

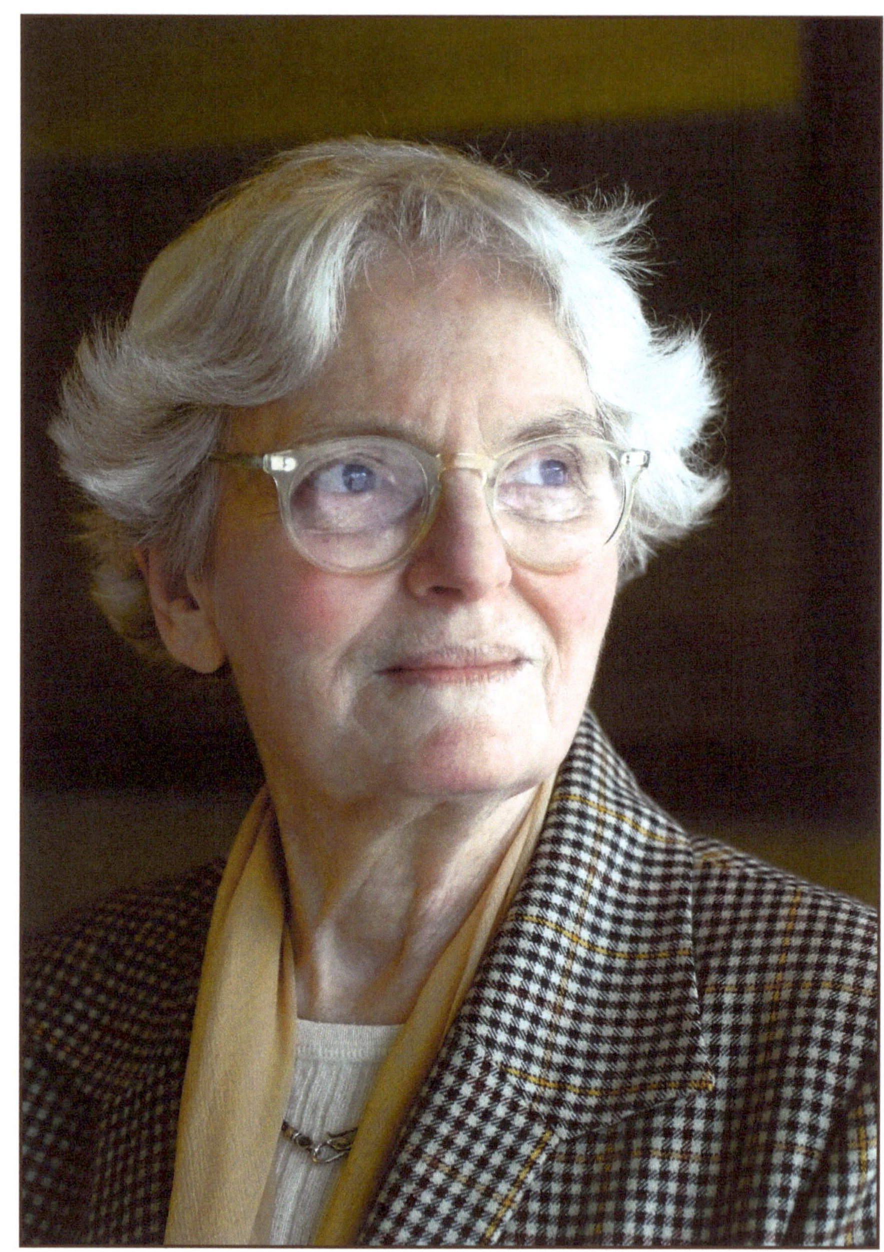

*Denise Scott Brown,* 2005 (Courtesy VSBA, Inc.)

*"A new openness in the minds and eyes of architects should help their ideals to be pragmatic ones and their utopias to be humane."*

*~ Denise Scott Brown from "Changing Family Forms,"* On Houses and Housing

(b. 1931)

# Denise Scott Brown

*Architect*

*Denise Scott Brown is an American architect, designer, urban planner, and the former principal and co-founder of the Philadelphia firm Venturi, Scott Brown and Associates. She was born in 1931 in Nkana, in the former British colony of Northern Rhodesia (now Zambia) and attended the University of the Witwatersrand in Johannesburg in 1952. She received her professional qualification in architecture at the Architectural Association School of Architecture in London in 1955 and emigrated to the United States in 1958. Brown obtained her Masters degrees of City Planning (1960) and Architecture (1965) from the University of Pennsylvania. Her husband, Robert Scott Brown, was also a student in this program but was killed in a car accident in 1959.*

*Brown stayed on as a faculty member at Penn for five years. She has also taught at the University of California (both Berkeley and Los Angeles campuses), Yale, and Harvard. She married fellow architect Robert Venturi in 1967. Brown worked as a principal at Venturi, Scott Brown and Associates, with Robert, until 2012.*

*Much of Brown's planning and design work has been in urban settings, including Philadelphia's South Street, Miami Beach, and Memphis. She also worked on the National Museum of the American Indian in Washington, DC, the Bouregreg Valley in Morocco, the Sainsbury Wing of the National Gallery in London, the Conseil Général complex in Toulouse, and the Mielparque Nikko Kirfuri Hotel and Spa in Japan. More recently, she has advised on the plan and design for the World Trade Center site and Penn's Landing in Philadelphia.*

*Her university campus planning projects include the Baker-Berry Library at Dartmouth, the Perelman Quadrangle at the University of Pennsylvania, the University of Michigan Life Sciences complex, and campus plans for Brown University and Tsinghua University in Beijing.*

*Brown is a postmodern architect whose influences stem from Africa, England, and Europe. She is known for her evolved method of combining planning and architecture. Her numerous projects and publications, along with her pedagogical influence on architectural and planning theory, have warranted her status as one of the most influential architects of the twentieth century.*

—Kara Cochran

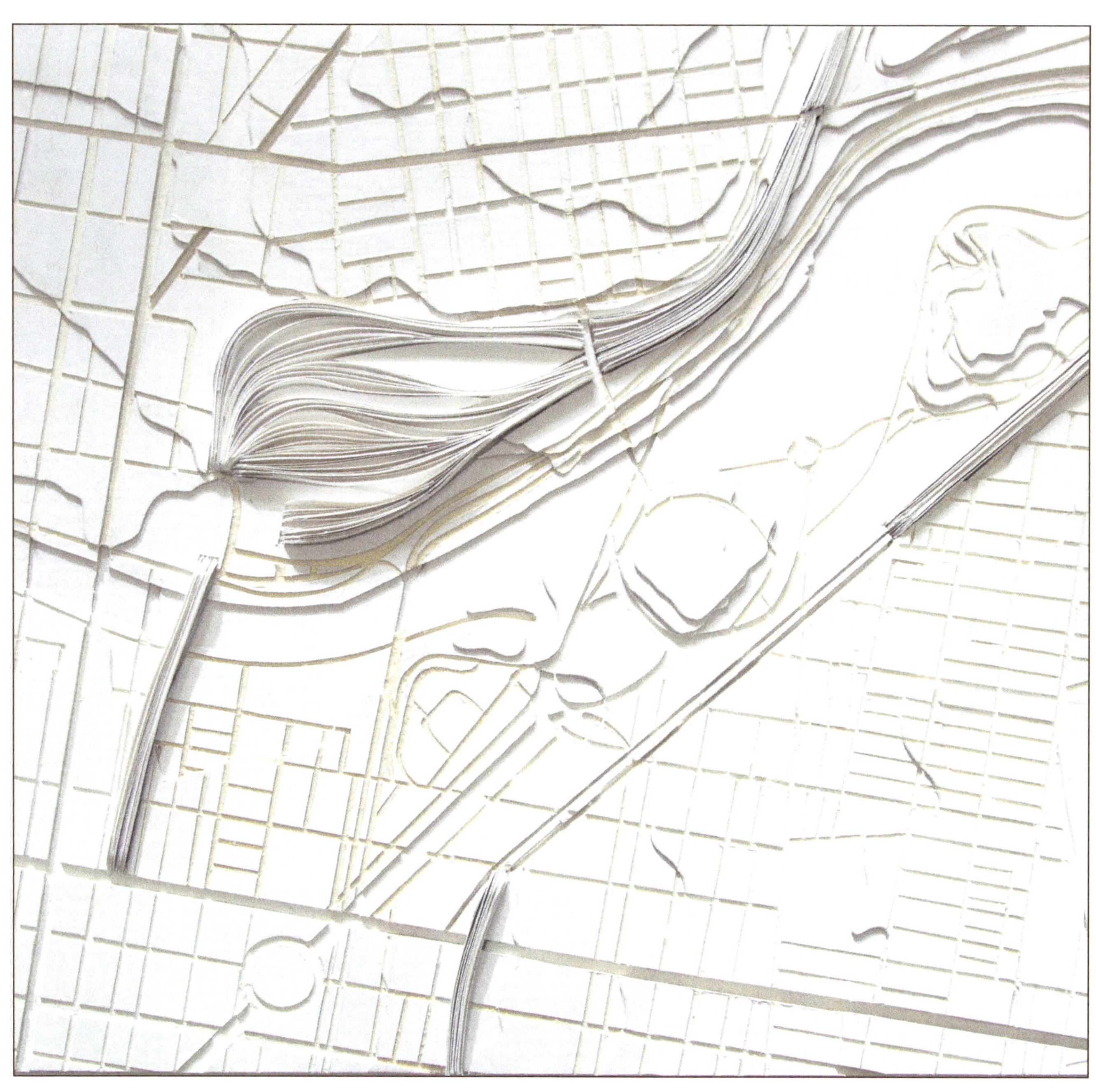

Dana Scott
*Reaction,* paper and board, 17 ¼" x 17 ¼"

Denise
Scott Brown

# NUMBER 9

M.H. Lorenzo

In the months after Sam died, once the parade of consolers trailed off, the house on Catharine Street went quiet. One afternoon Carmen came home from the spice shop, hung up her apron, and stared at the poker table now permanently folded against the living room wall. In the bathroom she looked at the two toothbrushes in their holder. The logical thing was to throw his out. Grief hit her gut in a sucker punch then, and she left both toothbrushes and walked out of the house.

"It's just a little beach house," Nancy said, "but it was designed by Robert Venturi. You can stay until it's demolished." As Carmen's old Toyota scraped up the sandy street, windows open to the salt breeze, she saw it clearly in the October dusk: a giant 9 on the door. Grateful tears slipped free as she shut off the engine. The house had been looking out for her.

The architect had built the living area upstairs for the ocean view and sunlight—a novelty in 1969. It was all white and awash in light from banks of windows and one giant sailboat-shaped window on the side. Carmen brought little to disrupt its white canvas. In the bathroom, a new toothbrush and towel, both white. The house wasn't insulated, Nancy had warned, and it got chilly at night. But in daytime, basking in sun, it was warm. This bright ungirded stretch of time offered no cleaning projects, no shifts at the spice shop, only dunes, sandy groves of pine, and trips to the grocery store. What had she done all these years? She'd knitted sweaters, planned vacations, gardened, cooked spectacular dinners. Twenty years had knitted themselves off in rows and then: a sudden binding off. The project finished. At night the great sailboat window shone moonlight on Carmen and asked a different question: What, now, would you like to become?

•

She bought a cheap easel and a sketchpad, although it had been twenty-five years since art school and she'd only dabbled since. She tried to sketch the view, but the pencil felt awkward in her hand and she flipped to a clean white page. It was November now, and the demolition date loomed closer. That night she had the first dream since August without Sam. She dreamed she woke and saw the sailboat window bobbing on waves of moonlight. Sketchpad under arm, she stepped into the window, and they set sail across the dark Atlantic sky.

In the morning she sketched a sailboat on the ocean, a woman steering.

•

Nancy sounded ecstatic. The house would be saved from the developer's wrecking ball. "Robert and Denise's son found someone who wants to put it on a barge and move it up to Long Island."

"Who's Denise?"

"Oh, Denise is his wife. She helped design the house."

Online at the café, Carmen found her: Denise Scott Brown, architect. Carmen noticed that Denise was involved in most of the works attributed to her more famous husband. The sailboat window, the huge number 9, the flood of seaside sun: whose mind had brought these into being?

•

The moving team would arrive in the frost of a January morning, tinkering at the foundation, calculating. Carmen would be gone, the little she'd lived with packed into the trunk of the Toyota, ready now to face the toothbrushes on Catharine Street. But come March she would wait at South Street Seaport to watch the little house sail through New York Harbor, her sketchpad open to its last blank page.

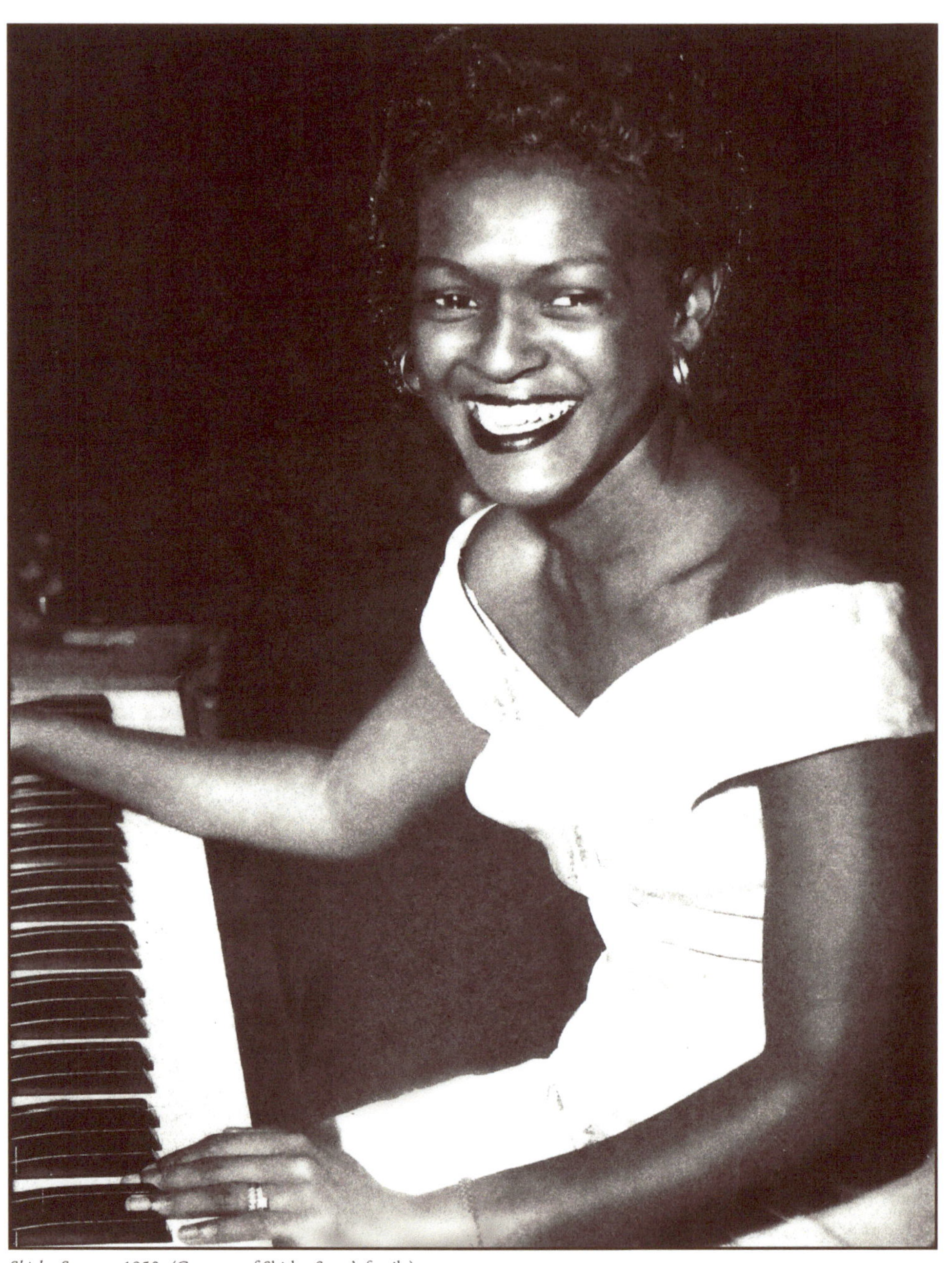

*Shirley Scott*, ca. 1950s (Courtesy of Shirley Scott's family)

*"The earliest remembrances I have of being on this planet are, one, sitting in my mother's lap in a rocking chair, and, two, playing the piano. I could always play. I could play before I ever took a lesson. That was something, I guess, given to me by God."*

*~ Shirley Scott*

(1934-2002)

## Shirley Scott

*Be-Bop Musician*

*Shirley Scott was an African-American jazz, soul, and be-bop organist known as "The Queen of the Organ" (a nickname derived from one of her albums). Born in Philadelphia, Scott showed an early interest in music and played the piano and trumpet. In the 1950s she played the organ in Philadelphia clubs and often performed with jazz great John Coltrane. Scott also particularly admired Jimmy Smith, who played the same Hammond B-3 electric organ.*

*Scott got her big break in the jazz world when she worked with Count Basie's tenor Eddie "Lock-jaw" Davis. They performed and recorded a series of "Cookbook" records with Prestige Records in the late 1950s, the biggest hit being 1958's "In the Kitchen." Scott launched her solo career that year and went on to record twenty-three additional records with Prestige between 1958 and 1964. She also worked with many other labels to record an additional twenty-two albums between 1963 and 1992.*

*Scott collaborated with many different musicians throughout her career, including tenor saxophonists Jimmy Forrest and Dexter Gordon, bassist George Duvivier, drummer Arthur Edgehill, vibraphonist Lem Winchester, and guitarist Kenny Burrell.* Blue Seven, *a collaboration with trumpeter Joe Newman and tenor saxophonist Oliver Nelson, includes memorable pieces such as "Give Me the Simple Life" and "Wagon Wheels."*

*Scott married soul-jazz saxophonist Stanley Turrentine in 1961. While their marriage ended in 1971, together they played and recorded* Hip Twist *and* Hip Soul *(1961),* Blue Flames *(1964), and* Soul Shoutin'.

*Scott went back to school at age fifty-seven to earn her BS degree, and toward the end of her career she became involved in music education. She taught jazz history at Cheyney University in the 1980s, was the music director at her church, and continued to perform locally in Philadelphia on the organ and piano. She was also musical director for Bill Cosby's* You Bet Your Life, *a remake of the classic quiz show that aired from 1992 to 1993.*

*The style of this remarkable woman, "The Queen of the Organ," has been described as an original, soulful, swinging, and rhythmic blend of blues, gospel, and be-bop.*

— Kara Cochran

# *Shirley Scott*

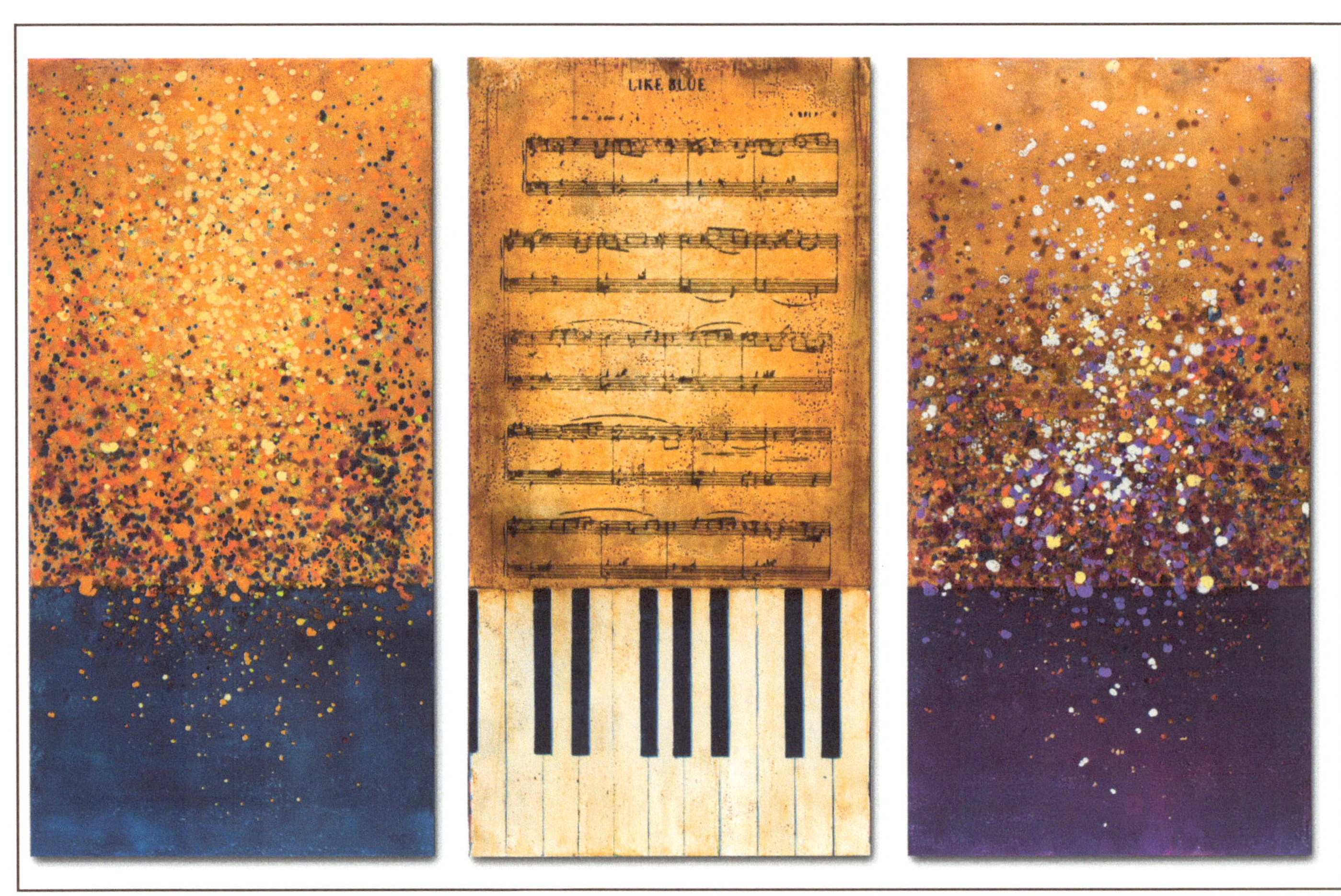


**Lisa Basil**
*Shirley Scott—Effervescence,* Triptych, encaustic and mixed media on panel, 23.75" x 35.25"

# RAINDROP BE BOP

Stefanie Levine Cohen

Matilda stepped gingerly from the beauty salon to her car, afraid of slipping on the leaves that covered the sidewalk after the morning rain. She hadn't missed her Friday-morning manicure, wash, and blowdry for thirty years. Even now, with nowhere to go and nobody to see except the mailman, she kept her appointment because it was her habit—and because she hoped that something exciting might happen, and she wanted to be ready.

The wind had picked up in the hour she'd spent inside the salon and it smelled like rain again. She slid carefully into the driver's seat of the silver Honda that had weathered to a dull gray. Eleven years and only twelve thousand miles. She sighed as she shut the door and removed the plastic head scarf and wiggled her feet. She'd been buying the same pair of black patent leather sandals, with the stubby one-inch heel and open toes so her bunions would fit, for years. She brushed a leaf off one of the toes now and shook her head. Her feet showed her seventy-eight years more than the rest of her.

She sat for a moment longer, hands in her lap, preparing to move on. She didn't notice the first drop of rain that fell against the roof of her car, or even the second but, by the fifth or sixth, she was attentive. She held her breath in the silence between the droplets. They started slowly, landing one at a time with a metallic thwack, then in couples and triples and dribbles and smacks, too many to count, a slow cascade that grew to a rumble. The pauses between raindrops drew her most. They were full, rich openings, teasing, demanding her attention. She tapped her foot in the spaces and jutted her jaw, dancing in place, joining in the syncopation of the rain until the drops came so quickly they obliterated the silence in a rapid onslaught of tiny pops. Her fingers drummed the steering wheel, arthritic knuckles tapping, freshly painted nails dancing. She was taken up, lost in the music, lost in the cocoon of the drops from the heavens that encircled her and joined her to the vast skies. She closed her eyes and swirled. The rain came faster, a timeless tune that changed by the moment and was gone before it landed. It was unstoppable. The song went on and on, different in each measure, building upon itself and turning a corner before taking a new direction. She followed along, willing to go where it took her, eager to follow an adventure of the heart and soul. The sound was her dance partner, the whole world her ballroom. Then, imperceptibly at first, the rain began to slow. An extra beat of silence replaced the drops that had thundered against the hard roof, and then another silent beat, and another. Soon, the spaces were bigger than the notes. The smell of musty autumn leaves came to Matilda's mind. Tapping toes eased, drumming fingers ceased their play. Matilda breathed deeply into the open space. Time had barely passed, or perhaps it had. She opened her eyes and lifted a hand to touch her hair. It was still in place. She started the engine and drove home.

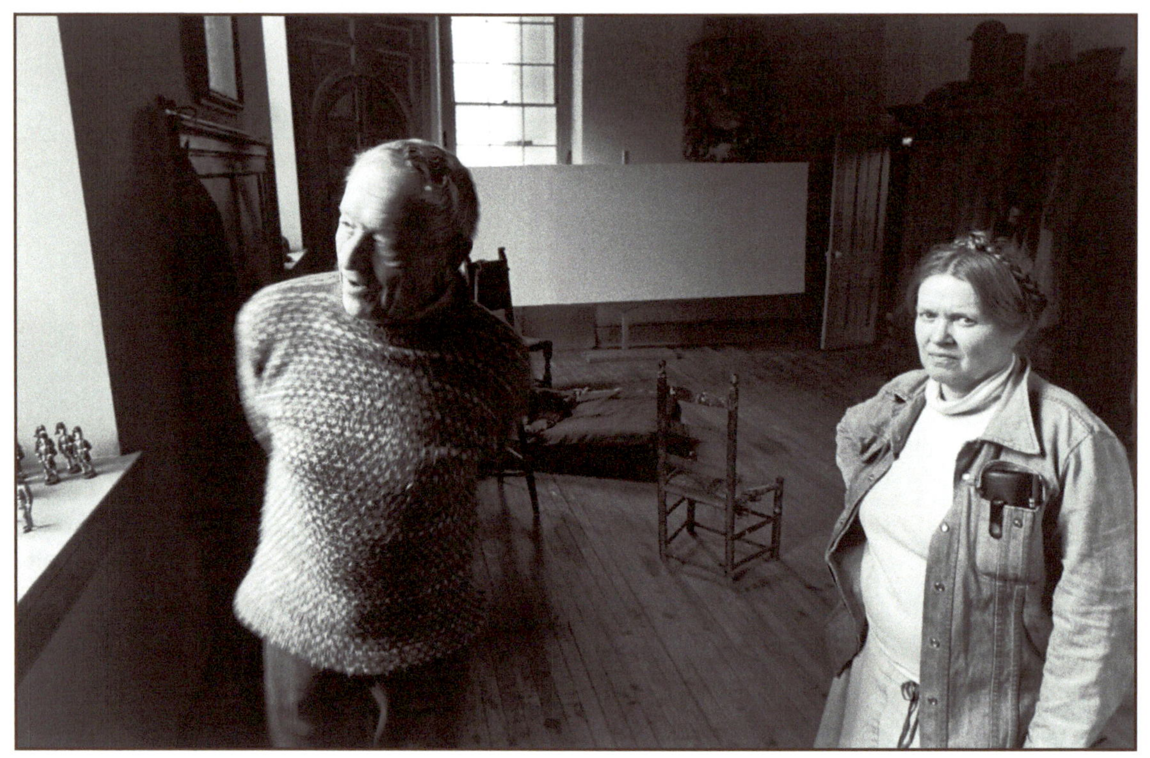

*Andrew Wyeth and Helga Testorf* (© David Alan Harvey/Magnum Photos)

*"The difference between me and a lot of painters is that I have to have a personal contact with my models. ... I have to become enamored. Smitten. That's what happened when I saw Helga walking up to the Kuerners' lane. She was this amazing, crushing blond."*

*~ Andrew Wyeth*

(b. 1939)

# Helga Testorf

*Muse*

*The Prussian-born Helga fled with her family to Demark in 1945 to escape the attacks of British and Soviet troops. They lived in refugee camps for several years and eventually moved back to Northern Germany. In 1955 Helga's father sent his daughter, age sixteen, to a Prussian Protestant convent. She left the convent when she became seriously ill and moved to Mannheim to study nursing. She married John Testorf, a naturalized American citizen, in 1958.*

*In 1961 the couple moved to Philadelphia and then to rural Chadds Ford, Pennsylvania, with their children. In Chadds Ford, Testorf was a caregiver for her neighbor Karl Kuerner, a friend and model to artist Andrew Wyeth.*

*Wyeth first drew Testorf in 1969. From 1971 to 1985, Helga Testorf was Wyeth's secret artistic muse. Throughout this fifteen-year period, the two met for sessions they kept hidden from both of their spouses. Wyeth captured Testorf in a variety of media—tempera, drybrush, watercolor, pencil—and he depicted her clothed and in the nude, in many different settings, and in every season. In all, this collection of works that was later titled "the Helga Pictures" comprises over 240 works of art. Testorf said, "I was lonely. He was at a point where he couldn't go any further in his work, and he sensed that. … I think we were both ready for what became a reality. It was inevitable."[1] Wyeth's renderings of Testorf convey the intimate connections between artist, muse, and setting.*

*When this collection was revealed to the public in 1986, the images of Testorf, with her striking German features and braided blond hair, caused a sensation. Testorf appeared on the cover of* Time *magazine in 1987 and of* Newsweek *in 1996. After a touring exhibition that attracted over a million visitors, the Helga pictures were sold to a private collector. The works themselves, as well as the secrecy and controversy surrounding their relationship, have made Testorf one of the world's most famous models and "the last person to be made famous by a painting."[2]*

— Rachel Mamola

[1] *Richard Meryman,* Andrew Wyeth: A Secret Life *(New York: Harper, 1998), p. 358.*

[2] *James Gardner, "A Villain in Pigtails,"* The New York Sun, *November 2, 2006.*

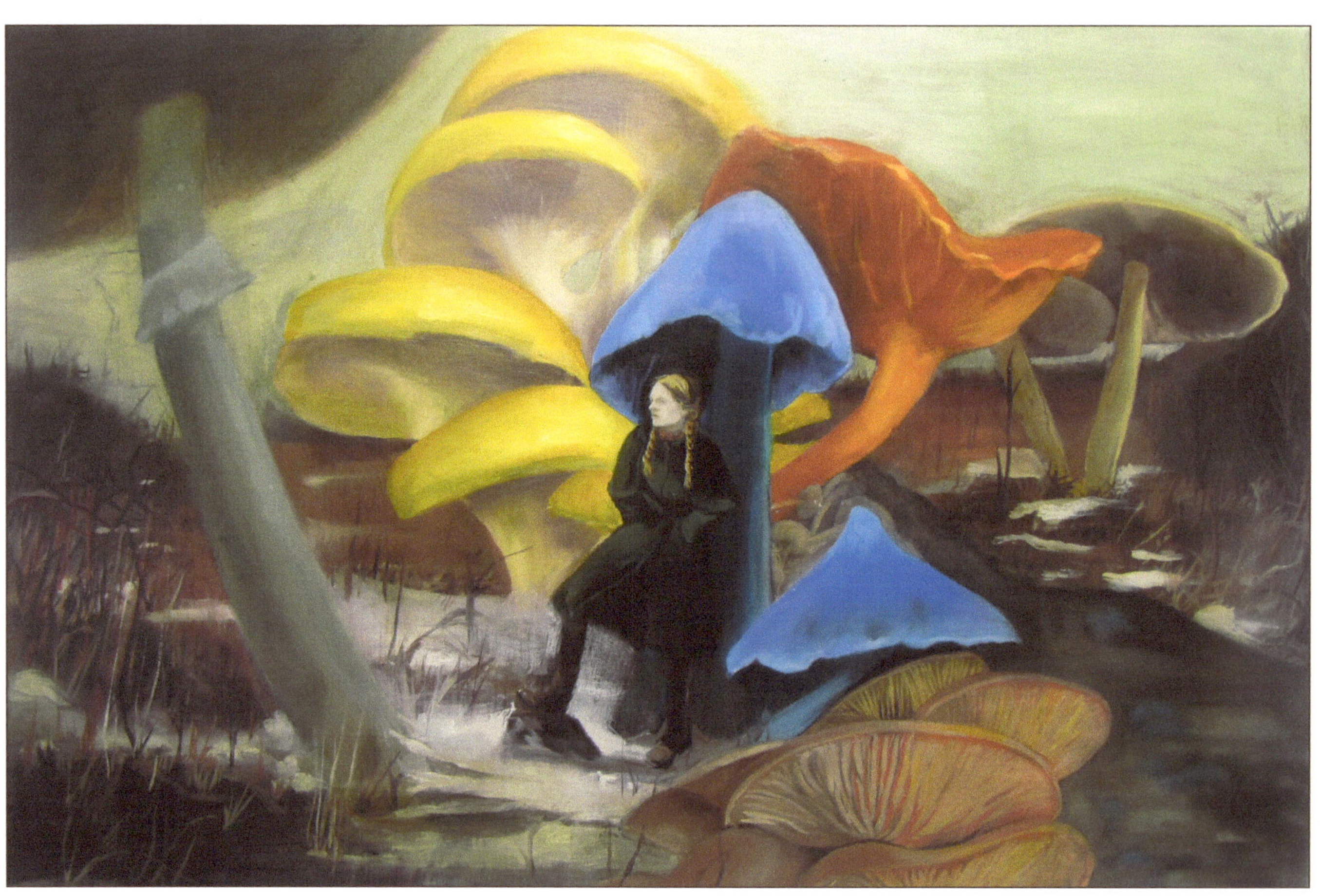

**Deirdre White**
*Helga in Wonderland,* oil on panel, 24" x 36"

Helga Testorf

# hausfrauthing

Pattie McCarthy

a road
a farm
a loden
coat the brave
a stride
the braid & against
grain     loden & wisp
& also the twist into
a wisp     hausfrauthing as
rückenfigur     slides
under you
assiduous     a stanza     under
oak tree understanding
a kenning slides
                    under you

her daughterthing skimmed
feathered faltered leafy     her hair
ribbon a flag     a wisp of a thing

*the many things that grow under*
*the corn stalks* & the back of her
head walking out of the corner of your eye
always an autumnthing when things
get pulpy leafy mixed together
a leaf & then leaves
out of the corner of mine eye

hausfrau is a whole vocabulary
                                        a domestic landscape
again & over                         dear
lovers in their beds I am
out the window on the hill

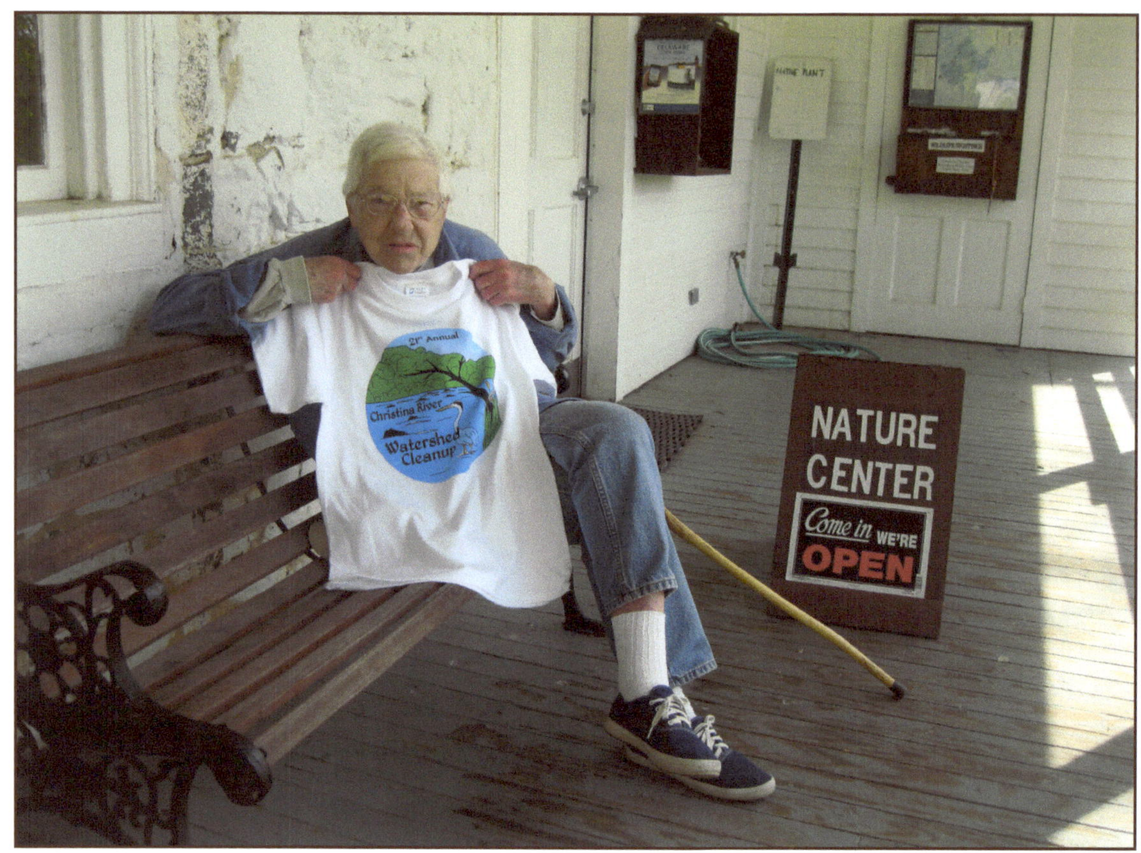


*Dorothy P. Miller* (Photograph by Angel Burns, courtesy of White Clay State Park, Delaware)

*"We had bumper stickers that gathered lots of attention ... You never really know what worked, so you have to do whatever you can think of. Individual acts themselves probably aren't enough; it probably takes all that you can think of to make it work."*

*~ Dorothy P. Miller*

(b. 1931)

## Dorothy P. Miller

*Environmentalist*

*Dorothy Miller was born in Windber, Pennsylvania and moved to Delaware in 1953. Her passion for bird watching led her to become one of Delaware's staunchest environmental activists. As a warbler fanatic, Miller spent many hours during the migration season in White Clay Creek State Park, which borders Pennsylvania and Delaware. In the late 1960s, Miller learned of a proposal to create a reservoir by damming the park's creek. Damming the creek would have flooded a thousand acres of land and destroyed countless plants and animals and their habitats. So Miller gathered data, organized a coalition of activists, lobbied politicians, and succeeded in saving most of the park.*

*But Miller's determination to save the environment didn't end there. For the next four decades, Miller continued to work tirelessly for various environmental causes. In 1971, Miller helped create the Coalition for Natural Stream Valleys, Inc., which advocates for the preservation and wise use of undeveloped land. She has also served as Delaware co-chair for the White Clay Creek Wild and Scenic River study. Before it became trendy, Miller encouraged everyone to recycle as much as possible. In addition, Miller organized park and creek cleanup days at White Clay. Miller is modest about her efforts and attributes the success of these endeavors to community support. Each person, she says, needs to consider his or her actions and the possible consequences for the environment.*

*In 1998, Delaware recognized Miller's preservation efforts by awarding her the Delaware Audubon Conservancy Award. Today, a seven-acre stretch of undeveloped land, named in her honor, runs through the White Clay Creek State Park where, every spring, Dorothy eagerly awaits the return of the warblers.*

— Nicole Contosta

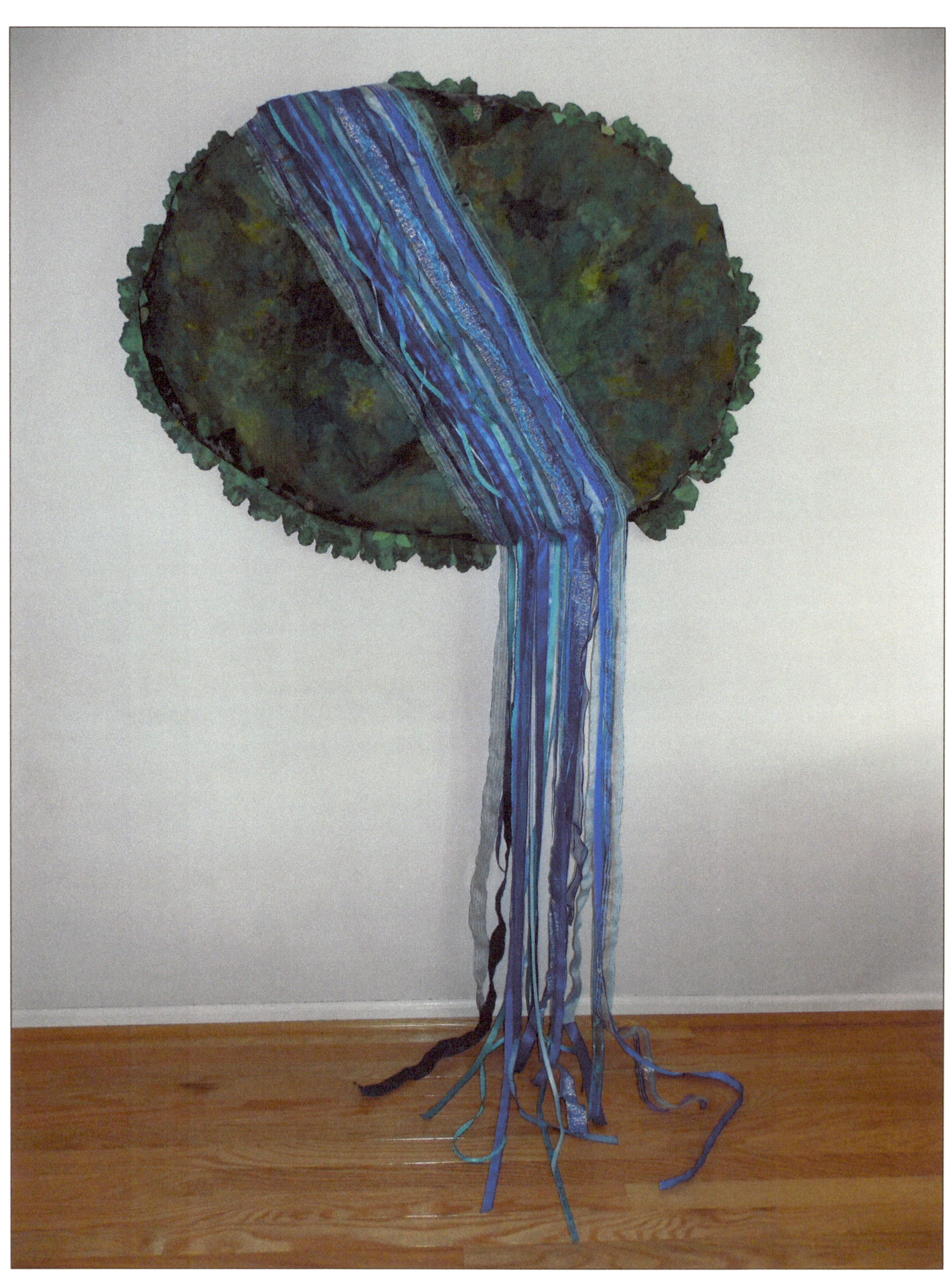

Karoline Wileczek
*Gifted Land of Flowing Water,* mixed media, 76" x 48" x 8"

Dorothy P. Miller

# UNDER

Ramona DeFelice Long

In an old science fiction tale, a man travels back in time to hunt a Tyrannosaurus Rex. A guide warns him not to wander from the path. The hunter is frightened by the huge magnificent creature he thought he wanted to kill. He runs away. Off the path, he crushes a butterfly under his boot. The future changes. A bad person rises to power. Even words mean different things.

***

Can a crushed butterfly change the future? Of course not. These things happen only in stories.

Don't they?

***

A bird watcher hears about plans to dam a local creek. The bird watcher is fond of warblers. She waits for their return each spring. Why warblers? They are not huge magnificent creatures, but the bird watcher enjoys their nest-building. She admires their industriousness and predictability.

The dam would damage the watershed where the warblers live.

The woman is outraged. She recalls the story of the hunter and the butterfly, of the future altered so even language is different, all because the small and the silent let a fascist have his way.

She doesn't look like a warrior, but that's not who she admires anyway. She admires warblers.

She arms herself with field notes about flora and fauna. She helps design a catchy bumper sticker that gets attention from people in parking lots. She lobbies politicians. She takes on counties and townships and companies on behalf of habitats and open spaces.

She wins. The dam is never built. The stream and the valley are under her protection. She watches her warblers and is just like them, industrious and predictable.

***

Did Dorothy P. Miller read "A Sound of Thunder" by Ray Bradbury? Did she equate her beloved birds with the butterflies, or see the dam as an evil politician, when she fought to preserve White Clay Creek? I have no clue.

A section of White Clay Creek State Park bears her name. I walk the trail through acres of undisturbed parkland, where the undammed creek meanders, and warblers return each spring.

I don't leave the path. Back at my car, I think of Ray Bradbury and Dorothy P. Miller and check under my boots.

# Contributors

## Sarah Josepha Hale *p. 8*

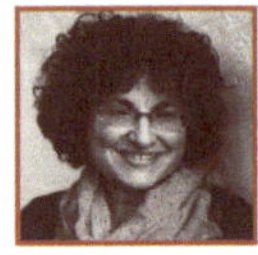

**ARTIST: Felise Luchansky** is an award-winning artist who exhibits in solo, juried, and invitational exhibitions throughout the Mid-Atlantic region. Her awards include an Individual Artist Fellowship in Works on Paper from the Delaware Division of the Arts. She is a member of InLiquid and was a participant in the Sketchbook Project, 2013, Brooklyn, NY. She recently co-curated "The White Cube," an international exhibit that traveled to London. Luchansky studied at the Pennsylvania Academy of the Fine Arts and holds a BA in Studio Art and Art History from Rutgers. www.feliseluchansky.com.

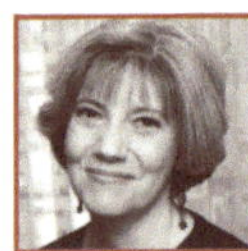

**AUTHOR: Tara S. Smith** is an MFA candidate in the Creative Writing program at Rosemont College. She is Program Director for PS Books and a freelance editor who has come to Philadelphia from Vermont, via Ireland.

## Lucretia Mott *p. 12*

**ARTIST: Rachel Dougherty** is a riproarin' Philadelphia illustrator, hailing from the northern suburbs and now residing a quick jaunt from the Rocky steps. Her stature may be diminutive but her clout is mighty. She works with acrylic paint and a vibrant sense of humor, and she is drawn to historical and educational subject matter. Her clients include Sterling Publishing, Port Discovery, Pennsylvania Real Estate Investment Trust, *Woman to Woman Magazine*, Resource Real Estate, Capstone Publishing (Picture Window Books), and the Annenberg School of Communication.

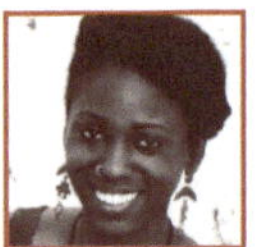

**POET: Alyesha Wise** ("Ms. Wise") is an international poet, speaker, teaching artist, and founder of the Philadelphia community arts organization "Love, Us." She is a two-time Women of the World Poetry Slam Finalist, and some of her other highlights include a 2012 interview with Ron Howard and being told by Russell Goings, co-founder of *Essence Magazine*, "In all, you are awesome." www.MsWiseDecision.com.

## Sarah Worthington Peter *p. 16*

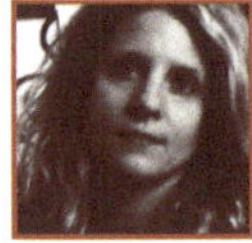

**ARTIST: Lisa T. Reed**, a regional artist, uses formal elements like line, shape, color, and pattern in her paintings, drawings, and sculptures to explore ideas about transformation, beauty, façade, and ritual. For more information on Reed's solo exhibition of her *Pattern Series* at The Artists' Gallery in Frederick, MD go to www.reedart.com.

**POET: Tamara Oakman** has won awards in poetry, fiction, memoir, and drama, is published in *Painted Bride Quarterly, Philadelphia Stories, Mad Poets Review*, and other magazines, has an MA in English and Humanities from Arcadia University, teaches Anne Sexton's poetry at Widener University, and is executive editor and co-founder of *Apiary Magazine*. www.apiarymagazine.com.

## Louisa May Alcott *p. 20*

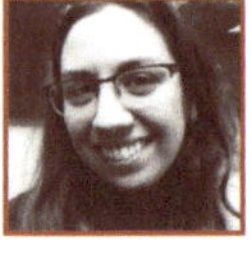

**ARTIST: Jessica Padilla,** a native of South Jersey, is a printmaker, painter, and educator. With a BFA in Art Education from Rowan University, Padilla has a wide interest in multimedia—from traditional printmaking techniques to unconventional approaches to a paint surface. In 2011, she received the Seward Johnson Consortium Travel Scholarship to study abroad in Florence, Italy. Her work has been shown in small galleries in New Jersey including the Perkins Center for the Arts, High Street Gallery, and the student gallery at Rowan University. In 2008, just before entering college, she received the New Jersey Governor's Award for Excellence in the Arts. At Rowan she received the Earl W. Hinton and Dolores Copeland Medallion Award for Volunteerism for her involvement with the Educational Opportunity Fund program and dedication to the continued academic success of young adults and future artists. She resides and works in New Jersey.

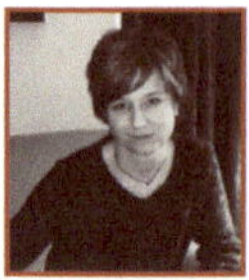

**AUTHOR: Nancy Kern** a New Jersey-born teacher and writer, holds an MFA from Sarah Lawrence College. Her work has appeared in *The Antioch Review* and *Prairie Schooner* and has been performed at the New Jersey Playwright's Theater in Millburn, NJ. Nancy has earned fellowships from the New Jersey Council on the Arts, the National Endowment for the Humanities, and the Geraldine Dodge Foundation. She has won numerous contests for her stories, including *Glimmer Train's* short story award for new writers and The Glenna Luschei *Prairie Schooner* Award. Nancy is currently at work on her first novel.

## Mary Cassatt *p. 24*

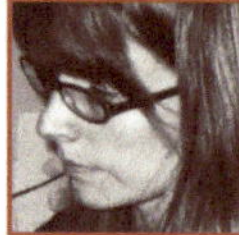

**ARTIST: Julia Rix** lives in Elkins Park and teaches art and ESL at Abington Junior High School. Her work has been published in *Philadelphia Stories* and exhibited in art centers throughout the Philadelphia area, including The Painted Bride Art Center, Abington Art Center, and the Philadelphia Sketch Club. She has organized numerous arts-based service learning projects and is a dedicated art education advocate. She is a member of several artist organizations, namely MamaCITA, Prints Link Philadelphia, and the American Color Print Society.

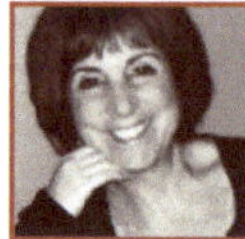

**POET: Liz Abrams-Morley**'s collection *Necessary Turns* was published by Word Press in 2010 and won an Eric Hoffer Award for Excellence in Small Press Publishing that year. Other collections include *Learning to Calculate the Half Life* (Zinka Press, 2001) and *What Winter Reveals* (Plan B Press, 2005). Her poems and short stories have been published in a variety of nationally distributed anthologies, journals, and ezines, and have also been read on NPR. Co-founder and co-director of *Around the Block Writing Collaborative* (www.aroundtheblockwriters.org), Liz is on the MFA faculty of Rosemont College and works with Philadelphia Public Schools' children in literacy through arts programs. Wife, mother, grandma, teacher, neighbor, sister, friend—Liz wades knee deep in the flow of everyday life from which she draws inspiration and, occasionally, exasperation.

## Lydia Morris *p. 28*

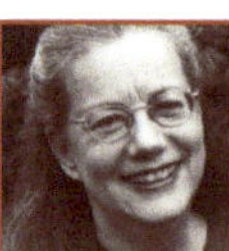

**ARTIST: Suzanne Comer** explores the use of digital photography as an art form and is especially known for using elements of her photographs to create award-winning photomontages. These works, as well as her unmanipulated photos, have been selected for exhibit in numerous juried shows. Suzanne studied with professional exhibiting artists while earning a BA in Fine Arts from California State University.

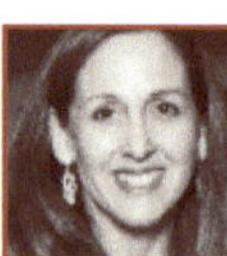

**POET: Christine Chiosi** writes poetry and short fiction. You can find her work in *Painted Bride Quarterly, The American Journal of Medical Genetics, Cloudbank, Apiary*, and other journals. Christine has lived in the greater Philadelphia area for many years. She is currently a graduate student in the Medical Humanities Program at Drew University, focusing her studies in the area of Narrative Medicine.

## Red Rose Girls *p. 32*

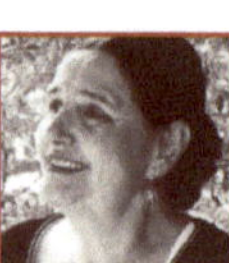

**ARTIST: Maria Keane** is a poet and fine artist with numerous memberships including The National League of American Pen Women (Art and Letters), the Chester County Art Association, and The National Gallery of Women Artists in Washington, DC, where her work is included in their archives. Various grants and awards include The Vermont Studio Center and Professional Artist Fellowship Grant from the Delaware Division of the Arts and the National Endowment for the Arts. Her watercolor, printmaking, and digital art have received distinctions nationally and locally. Keane is a published poet whose work can be found in the *Fox Chase Review*. Her paintings, prints, and illustrations are in private and corporate collections all across the area. She received

# Contributors

an undergraduate degree from Hunter College, City University of NY, and an MA from the University of Delaware (Phi Kappa Phi) and was an Adjunct Professor of Fine Arts at Wilmington University from 1984 to 2009.

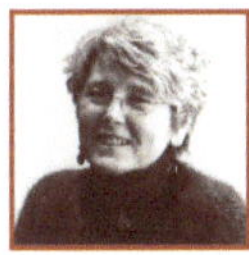

**POET: Nathalie F. Anderson** has authored three books: *Following Fred Astaire*, which won the 1998 Washington Prize from The Word Works; *Crawlers*, which won the 2005 McGovern Prize from Ashland Poetry Press; and *Quiver*, published in 2011 by Penstroke Press. She has authored libretti for three operas—*The Black Swan; Sukey in the Dark*; and an operatic version of Arthur Conan Doyle's *A Scandal in Bohemia*—all in collaboration with the composer Thomas Whitman and Orchestra 2001 in Philadelphia. A 1993 Pew Fellow, she serves currently as Poet in Residence at the Rosenbach Museum and Library, and she teaches at Swarthmore College, where she is a Professor in the Department of English Literature and directs the Program in Creative Writing.

## Violet Oakley

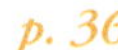

*p. 36*

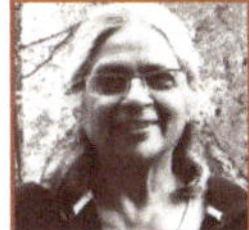

**ARTIST: Geeta N. Ahya** is a self-taught digital artist. She creates her beautiful artwork using Adobe Photoshop, Adobe Illustrator, and photographs. She developed her interest in digital art while designing websites. She has designed websites for non-profits, small businesses, artists, and teachers. Before becoming a web designer, Geeta worked for many years in information technology as a programmer/database developer. She holds a master's degree in management from Lesley College in Massachusetts.

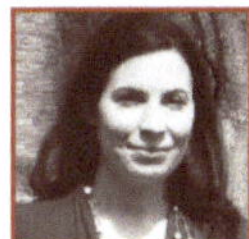

**POET: Laura L. Buenzle** holds her MFA from Rosemont College. She lives in suburban Philadelphia and primarily writes about art and artists.

## Marian Anderson

*p. 40*

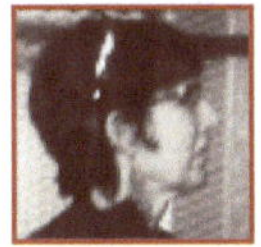

**ARTIST: Lesley Mitchell** was educated in the fine arts at Arts High School in Newark, NJ, Douglass College, and the Pennsylvania Academy of the Fine Arts, where she trained in painting and printmaking. She has taught printmaking and works on paper classes at PAFA and other regional institutions and currently teaches works on paper classes privately. She shows her artist's books, works on paper, and paintings on panel nationally and internationally.

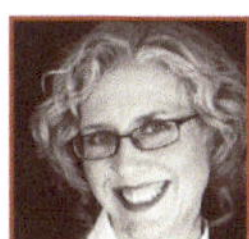

**AUTHOR: Carla (C.J.) Spataro** is the Director of the MFA in Creative Writing program at Rosemont College. She is also the Editorial Director and co-publisher of *Philadelphia Stories* magazine and PS Books. She is a Pennsylvania Council on the Arts fellowship winner for fiction. Her short stories can be read in a number of literary journals including *Painted Bride Quarterly, Wild River Review, XConnect, The Baltimore Review, Mason's Road, and 4' 33"* (an online audio journal based in London). Nominated for a Million Writer's South Award, she also was twice named a finalist in the Philadelphia City Paper Fiction contest and was a finalist in the Mason's Road contest.

## Alice Neel

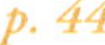

*p. 44*

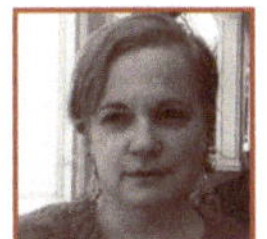

**ARTIST: Melissa Tevere**, primarily a landscape and portrait painter, graduated from Tyler School of Art with her BFA in painting. Recent exhibitions include a group exhibition at the Rotunda at the Pennsylvania State Capital in Harrisburg, November 2013, "MamaCITA at the Painted Bride," Philadelphia, January 2013, and "Forgotten Philadelphia," at the Fairmount Park Welcome Center, Philadelphia, September 2012. Her work is on permanent display at the MPB Apartments, Mission First, Philadelphia and the Women's Center of Einstein Memorial Hospital, Norristown. Tevere is also the art editor of *Philadelphia Stories,* co-owner of Conway Collision, and the founder of MamaCITA. www.mamacitaarts.com.

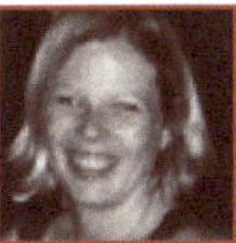

**AUTHOR: Nicole Contosta** received her MFA from Rosemont College in 2012. She works as a general assignment staff reporter for the *Weekly Press* and the *University City Review*.

## Margaret Mead

*p. 48*

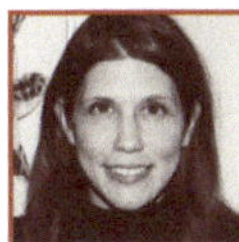

**ARTIST: Heather Devlin Knopf** is an artist, writer, and children's book illustrator who has a passion for exploring social change through education and the arts. In 2013, Little Pickle Press published Knopf's first illustrated picture book (written by Diana Prichard), and she is working on future projects with The Andrea Brown Literary Agency. A business graduate from Carnegie Mellon University, Knopf recently earned her MFA through the Hartford Art School at the University of Hartford. She received a graduate study grant to research her thesis picture book project in Paris, which greatly influenced her ideas about story. Heather is a member of MamaCITA and the Society of Children's Book Writers and Illustrators. Her acrylic paintings and monotype pieces have been exhibited in solo and group shows throughout the Philadelphia area. Knopf lives in Elkins Park with her family and has two young, highly imaginative, boys.

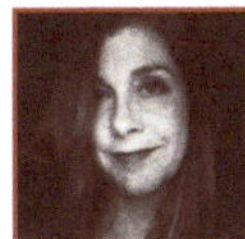

**AUTHOR: Julie Odell** has published short stories in journals such as the *Berkeley Fiction Review, Five Chapters*, and *Atticus Review*. She was a 2004 MacDowell Colony fellow and has recorded personal commentary for NPR. She holds an MA from the Center for Writers at the University of Southern Mississippi and teaches English at the Community College of Philadelphia. She is currently working on a novel.

## Ruth Robinhold

*p. 52*

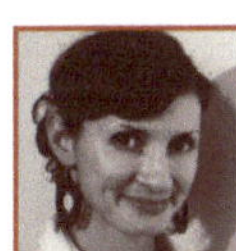

**ARTIST: Michelle Ciarlo-Hayes** is an award-winning photographer and digital artist who uses many techniques (traditional film, antique viewfinders, collage, and painting) to bring her visions to life. Her work has been exhibited in a number of venues, including the City Hall (Philadelphia), the Pennsylvania State Capitol (Harrisburg, PA), and the University of Oxford (UK), and numerous galleries and boutiques across North America carry her artwork and home accessories. She lives just outside Philadelphia with her husband, two young boys, and two very badly behaved dogs. mkcphotography.com.

**POET: Carol Rabuck** is an artist and writer living in Philadelphia. She makes a living in sales and technical support and has a BFA from Virginia Commonwealth University. She has also been a frequent attendee of the poetry workshops at University of the Arts. She has a lifelong fascination with boats, rowing, canoeing, and water.

## Edna Andrade

*p. 56*

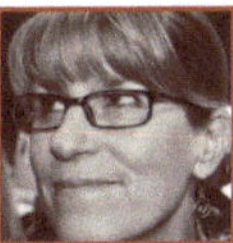

**ARTIST: Karen Hunter McLaughlin** is a lifelong Philadelphia artist working in many mediums. Karen's most recent work is the multi-year, critically acclaimed, collaboration One Year. One Year is an art installation consisting of hundreds of sculptural steel wire vessels. It addresses the apathy of urban communities in areas of high violent crime. One Year was a collaboration with four women, co-members of MamaCITA, and was funded in part by several Leeway Art and Change Grants. This monumental exhibit was installed in venues around the city during 2013 and was part of the Philadelphia FringeArts Festival.

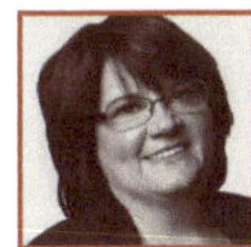

**AUTHOR: Tori Bond** is an MFA candidate in the Creative Writing program at Rosemont College. She earned a BA in English at Rutgers University and received the G. Stuart Demarest Memorial Award for academic excellence. Her flash fiction has appeared in *Flash Fiction Funny, Monkey Bicycle, Wilderness House Literary Review, Every Day Fiction, Hoot,* and others. In addition to writing short, short stories, she is also working on a satirical novel. A native of New Jersey, she now lives in Bucks County, PA with her husband and two children.

# Contributors

## Alice Steer Wilson p. 60

**ARTIST: Carol King Hood** has painted in oil since childhood. She attended the Philadelphia College of Art, worked as a designer in the graphics arts business, and raised four children. Carol lives in Cape May, NJ where she is a Grumbacher instructor and offers classes and private art lessons for adults and children. She is a member of the Oil Painters of America and shows her work in numerous exhibits in South Jersey and the Cape May area. www.carolkinghood.net.

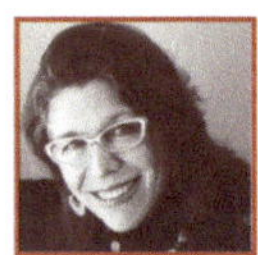

**POET: Janice Wilson Stridick**'s writing appears in *Arts & Letters, Boxcar Poetry Review, Dos Passos Review, Louisville Review, Schuylkill Valley Journal*, and many more. She has reviewed books and art for *NY Arts Magazine, Philadelphia Stories*, and *Cape May Star and Wave*. In 1992, she launched Southbound Press and served as editor and publisher of *The View In Winter*, a three-generation work of art and poetry. She graduated from the Annenberg School of the University of Pennsylvania, earned an MFA in writing from Vermont College, and has taught in Rutgers University's Writing Program and the Graduate Publishing Program at Rosemont College. Her poem "Homecoming" won the Lois Cranston Prize from Calyx Press, and her book, *Alice Steer Wilson: Light, Particularly* was released nationally in 2013. She lives in southern New Jersey with her delightful architect husband and one cranky cat. www.janicewilsonstridick.com.

## Denise Scott Brown p. 64

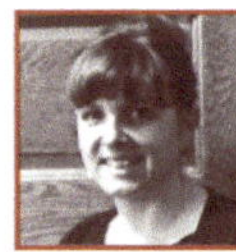

**ARTIST: Dana Scott** is a multi-disciplinary artist working in the Philadelphia area. Her work is about observation, discovery, and detail. It is inspired by natural form, pattern, and the beauty within simplicity. She received a master's degree from Tyler School of Art, Temple University and a bachelor's degree from Rhode Island School of Design. She has exhibited both nationally and internationally and has received numerous awards, including a University Fellowship from Temple University and a Fulbright Fellowship to the Czech Republic. She is currently a visiting assistant professor at Philadelphia University and lives with her husband and two sons in Elkins Park.

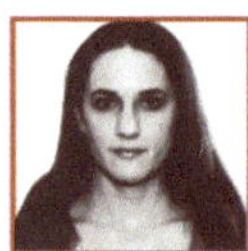

**AUTHOR: M.H. Lorenzo** lives and writes in Philadelphia. She believes that art, in its many forms, makes life worthwhile.

## Shirley Scott p. 68

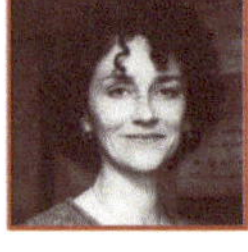

**ARTIST: Lisa Basil** was born in Buffalo, NY and currently resides in Norristown, PA. She studied graphic design and music at Jacksonville University before transferring to Moore College of Art and Design, where she received her BFA in printmaking in 1991. Since graduating, Basil has worked in various media including oil, acrylic, sculpture, and photography. She now predominantly works in encaustic and mixed media. Her work can be found in both private and public collections including those of the McGraw-Hill Companies, MasterCard, and the law firm of Wapner Newman Wigrizer Brecher & Miller. Lisa has been in numerous group and solo shows and she is the recipient of several awards, most recently the Yvonne M. Kelly Memorial Prize for Mixed Media from the Woodmere Art Museum in Philadelphia.

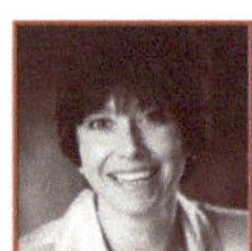

**AUTHOR: Stefanie Levine Cohen** studies and writes about birth, death, afterlife, and the human condition. She is working on a collection of short stories exploring these topics. Stefanie also works as a volunteer visitor for Samaritan Hospice in Marlton, NJ. She received her bachelor's and master's degrees in English from the University of Pennsylvania and her JD from the New York University School of Law. Stefanie is a long-time member of the Rittenhouse Writers Group in Philadelphia. Her work has been published in *The Montreal Review* and the *Green Hills Literary Lantern* and is forthcoming in *ginosko* and *The MacGuffin*. Stefanie lives in Cherry Hill, NJ with her husband and their three teenaged daughters.

## Helga Testorf p. 72

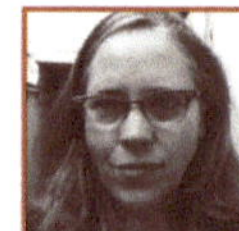

**ARTIST: Deirdre White** received a BFA in painting and drawing from Tyler School of Art in Philadelphia and an MFA in Studio Art from UC Davis, where she was a Chandler Graduate Fellow. Her paintings have been exhibited across the country, as well as in Copenhagen. She was raised in both California and Pennsylvania, and her paintings are disjointed personal narratives that address themes of loss, exposure, erosion, and the weight of our collective anxieties. She is interested in the concept of nature as a socially constructed place, and in landscape as a metaphor for psychological space. She currently teaches a collaborative design course at the City College of San Francisco.

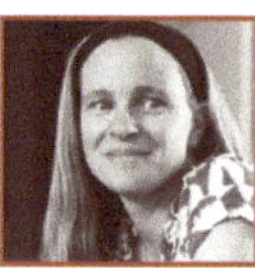

*Photo © Colin Lenton*

**POET: Pattie McCarthy** is the author of six books of poetry, most recently *Marybones* (Apogee Press) and the forthcoming *Nulls* (Horse Less Press) and *Quiet Book* (Apogee). A 2011 Pew Fellow in the Arts, she was an artist resident at the Elizabeth Bishop House in Great Village, Nova Scotia in summer 2013. She teaches at Temple University.

## Dorothy P. Miller p. 76

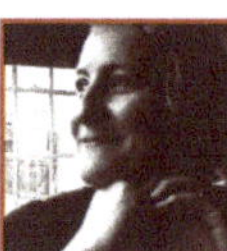

**ARTIST: Karoline Wileczek** lives and keeps a studio in Newark, DE along with her husband and two young children. Her work has been shown at the Minneapolis Institute of Art, the Delaware Center for the Contemporary Arts, the Biggs Museum of Art, The Soap Factory, MN, and various art centers and galleries nationally. Her work is owned by private collectors across the country and in Latin America. She holds an MFA in Painting from the University of Minnesota and a BFA from Tyler School of Art, Temple University. Recent awards have included a Delaware Division of the Arts Fellowship in Painting and an opportunity grant from the D.D.O.A. *Photo © Dragonfly Leathrum*

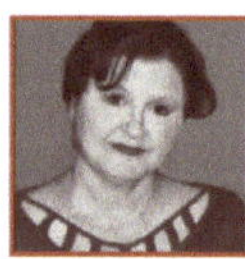

**AUTHOR: Ramona DeFelice Long**'s writing has appeared in publications including *The Arkansas Review, TOSKA, Literary Mama, CRICKET, 10kToBI, Handspun, Delaware Beach Life*, and *Blue Lit*. She has been awarded fellowships and scholarships from the Mid-Atlantic Arts Foundation, the Virginia Center for the Creative Arts, the Delaware Division of the Arts, the Pennsylvania State Arts Council, the Society of Children's Book Writers and Illustrators, *Philadelphia Stories*, and the Rehoboth Beach Writers' Guild. Her day job is as an independent editor and online writing instructor. She lives in Delaware and maintains a literary blog at ramonadef.wordpress.com.

## Research

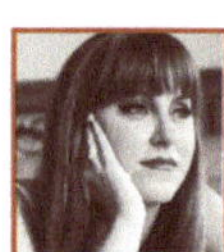

**Kara Cochran** is in her first year of the MFA program in Creative Writing at Rosemont College. Her pre-MFA work consists of a collection of narrative war poems titled "Memoranda." She has lived in Philadelphia for two years and is proud to call it home.

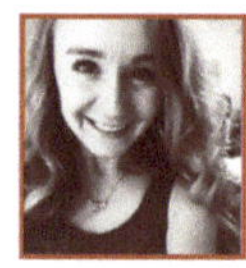

**Rachel Mamola** is an undergraduate Writing Arts student at Rowan University. She currently interns at *Philadelphia Stories* and works as a sports photographer at the Rowan University Sports Information Office. She hopes to pursue a degree in publishing and to one day illustrate and write books for children and young adults.

**Additional research** for this volume by Tori Bond, Nicole Contosta, Tara S. Smith, and Melissa Tevere.

## Design

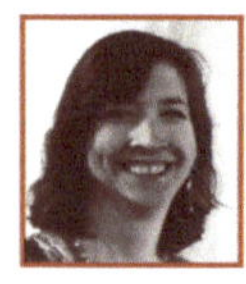

**Sue Harvey** graduated with a BFA in Graphic Arts from Kent State University. After working in the industry for several years, she struck out on her own and created Vignette Visual Media. Since 1993, Sue has been providing design services for many diverse clients in the Philadelphia area. Sue lives in Elkins Park with her husband and two daughters.

# Sources


## Sarah Josepha Hale

Finley, Ruth Elbright. *The Lady of Godey's, Sarah Josepha Hale*. Philadelphia: J. B. Lippincott Company, 1931.

Greenberg, Hope. *Godey's Lady's Book:* "Sarah Josepha Hale." Sept. 2001. uvm.edu/~hag/godey/hale.html.

Hale, Sarah Josepha. *The New Household Receipt-Book*. Philadelphia, 1853.

—. *The Ladies' Wreath*. Boston: Marsh, Capen & Lyon, 1837.

Lewis, Jone Johnson. "Sarah Josepha Hale: Editor, *Godey's Lady's Book*." womenshistory.about.com/od/godeyshale/a/Sarah-Josepha-Hale.htm.

## Lucretia Mott

Cromwell, Otelia. *Lucretia Mott*. Cambridge: Harvard University Press, 1958.

"Lucretia Mott." *About.com Women's History*. womenshistory.about.com/od/suffragepre1848/p/lucretia_mott.htm.

"Lucretia Mott: Biography." *Bio.com*. A&E Networks. biography.com/people/lucretia-mott-9416590.

## Sarah Worthington Peter

McAllister, A.S. *In Winter We Flourish: Life and Letters of Sarah Peter*. New York: Longmans, Green and Co., 1939.

"Sarah Worthington Peter." *Moore College of Art and Design*. moore.edu/about-moore/mission-history/sarah-worthington-peter.

## Louisa May Alcott

"Louisa May Alcott." *Poet's Corner*. theotherpages.org/poems/poem-ab.html#alcott.

"Louisa May Alcott." *Empirezine*. empirezine.com/spotlight/alcott/alcott.htm.

Merriman, C.D. "Louisa May Alcott (1832–1888)." *Online-Literature*. online-literature.com/alcott/.

*New York Times*. "On This Day: March 7, 1888. Louisa May Alcott Dead." nytimes.com/learning/general/onthisday/bday/1129.html.

## Mary Cassatt

Gerdts, William H. *American Impressionism*. New York: Abbeville, 2001.

Johnson Lewis, Jone. "Mary Cassatt." *About.com Women's History*. womenshistory.about.com/od/cassattmary/a/mary-cassatt.htm.

Wood, James N. *Impressionism and Post-impressionism in the Art Institute of Chicago*. Easthampton, MA: Hudson Hills, 2000.

## Lydia Morris

"Ode to Lydia." *Morris Arboretum Online Archives*. business-services.upenn.edu/arboretum/archives/HistoricPDF/2012-7-2-OdetoLydia.pdf.

Pape, C., ed. *Always Growing: The Story of the Morris Arboretum*. Philadelphia, 2010.

Rivinus, Mrs. E.F., and Mrs. F.W. Morris. "A History of the Morris Arboretum." *Morris Arboretum Online Archives*. business-services.upenn.edu/arboretum/archives/HistoricPDF/2011-13-1ArbHistory1975.pdf.

## Red Rose Girls

Carter, Alice A. *The Red Rose Girls: An Uncommon Story of Art and Love*. New York: Harry Abrams, 2000.

Gury, Al. "Ancestral Pioneers: Women who Set the Course." *Per Contra*. Summer 2006. percontra.net/archive/3gurypioneers.htm.

## Violet Oakley

"Biography of Violet Oakley." *Delaware Art Museum*. delart.org/collections/HFS_library/finding_aids/Violet%20Oakley%20Papers#Bio.

Elzea, Rowland, and Elizabeth H. Hawkes, eds. *A Small School of Art: The Students of Howard Pyle*. Wilmington: Delaware Art Museum, 1980.

"The Red Rose Girls: An Uncommon Story of Art and Love." *USA Today Magazine* 132 (2004): 34–37.

"Violet Oakley." *National Women's History Project*. nwhp.org/whm/oakley_bio.php.

## Marian Anderson

Keiler, Allan. *Marian Anderson: A Singer's Journey*. Champaign, IL: University of Illinois Press, 2000.

"Marian Anderson: A Dream, a Life, a Legacy." *Marian Anderson Historical Society*. mariandersonhistoricalsociety.weebly.com/biography.html.

"The Most Celebrated Contralto of the Twentieth Century." *The Marian Anderson Award*. mariandersonaward.org/?gclid=CPT-_rX_sroCFZSk4AoddA4A8Q#/index.php/marian-anderson.

## Alice Neel

"Alice Neel." *Alice Neel Estate*. aliceneel.com/biography.

Searle, Adrian. "The Weird World of Alice Neel." *The Guardian*. July 2010. theguardian.com/artanddesign/2010/jul/07/alice-neel.

## Margaret Mead

Lutkehaus, Nancy C. *Margaret Mead: The Making of an American Icon*. Princeton: Princeton University Press, 2008.

"Margaret Mead 1901–1978." *Anthropology*. University of South Florida. anthropology.usf.edu/women/mead/margaret_mead.htm.

Shankman, Paul. *The Trashing of Margaret Mead: Anatomy of an Anthropological Controversy*. Madison: University of Wisconsin Press, 2009.

# Sources


## Ruth Robinhold

Josephs, Ira. "Rowing their Own Way: Ruth Robinhold Secured a Place for Women on Boathouse Row 65 Years Ago." *Philly.com.* June 17, 2003. articles.philly.com/2003-06-17/sports/25448270_1_boathouse-row-undine-barge-club-honorary-member.

Morrison, John F. "Ruth Adams Robinhold, 99, Rowing Pioneer." *Philly.com.* December 18, 2012. articles.philly.com/2012-12-18/news/35892852_1_women-rowing-quad-races-ruth-robinhold-trophy.

Robinhold, Ruth. Interview by Michelle Ciarlo-Hayes. 2001.

## Edna Andrade

"Edna Andrade Optical Paintings 1960–1966." *Locks Gallery.* Jan. 12, 2007. locksgallery.com/exhibits_works.php?eid=43.

Paschall, W. Douglass. "The Romantic Geometer." In *Sensational Edna Andrade's Drawings.* Philadelphia: Woodmere Art Museum, 2007.

Rosenberg, Amy. "An Outpouring of Art." *Philly.com.* Sept. 14, 2012. articles.philly.com/2012-09-14/news/33818374_1_edna-andrade-locks-gallery-sueyun-locks.

Rubalevskaya, Julia. "Art Exhibit Gets Rave Reviews." *The Daily Pennsylvanian.* Jan. 21, 2003. thedp.com/index.php/article/2003/01/art_exhibit_gets_rave_reviews.

Sozanski, Edward J. "Esteemed Phila. Artist Andrade Dies." *Philly.com.* April 18, 2008. articles.philly.com/2008-04-18/news/25251484_1_addison-gallery-art-museum-fine-arts.

## Alice Steer Wilson

"Alice Steer Wilson." *Alice Steer Wilson.* alicesteerwilson.com/about.html.

Fox, Karen. "The Painter and the Poet." *CapeMay.com.* capemay.com/magazine/2012/12/the-painter-and-the-poet.

Hagenmayer, S. Joseph. "Alice Steer Wilson." *Philly.com.* articles.philly.com/2001-07-25/news/25316006_1_oil-painting-watercolor-shore.

Wasserman, Burton. "Cape May Captured Brilliantly, Warmly, in New Book on Artwork of Alice Steer Wilson." *montgomerynews.com.* Oct. 8, 2013. montgomerynews.com/articles/2013/10/08/entertainment/doc52541a9addd1a967961484.txt.

Wilson Stridick, J. *Alice Steer Wilson: Light, Particularly.* Merchantville, NJ: Southbound Press, 2013.

—. Email interview by Rachel Mamola. Oct. 2013.

## Denise Scott Brown

"Architect to Receive Radcliffe Medal: Denise Scott Brown Honored at Radcliffe Day Luncheon." *Harvard Gazette.* news.harvard.edu/gazette/2005/06.09/15-radmedal.html.

"Denise Scott Brown." *IAWA.* lumiere.lib.vt.edu/iawa_db/view_all.php3?person_pk=343®ion=&table=bio&cSel=.

"Robert Venturi and Denise Scott Brown." *Archinomy.* archinomy.com/case-studies/264/robert-venturi-and-denise-scott-brown.

Stephens, Suzanne. "Newsmakers: Denise Scott Brown and Robert Venturi." *Architectural Record.* archrecord.construction.com/news/2012/07/120725-Newsmaker-Denise-Scott-Brown.asp.

Tamas, Andrea. "Interview: Robert Venturi and Denise Scott Brown." *Arch Daily.* archdaily.com/130389/interview-robert-venturi-denise-scott-brown-by-andrea-tamas/.

## Shirley Scott

"Scholarship Named for Renowned Jazz Organist, Shirley Scott, to Benefit CU Music Students." *Cheney University.* June 22, 2012. cheyney.edu/pr/news/23491/5700/no.

"Shirley Scott." *Concord Music.* concordmusicgroup.com/artists/Shirley-Scott/.

Shirley Scott." *last.fm.* last.fm/music/Shirley+Scott.

"Shirley Scott, 67, Performer Known as the Queen of the Organ." March 16, 2002. *The New York Times.* nytimes.com/2002/03/16/arts/shirley-scott-67-performer-known-as-the-queen-of-the-organ.html.

## Helga Testorf

"American Painter Andrew Wyeth Dies at 91." *today.com.* Jan. 16, 2009. today.com/id/28690990#.UmptCnCkrnE.

"Andrew and Helga." *Museworthy.* Aug. 31, 2008. artmodel.wordpress.com/2008/08/31/andrew-and-helga/.

Gardner, James. "A Villain in Pigtails." *The New York Sun,* Nov. 2, 2006.

Jiminez, Jill Berk. *Dictionary of Artists' Models.* London: Fitzroy Dearborn, 2001.

Meryman, Richard. *Andrew Wyeth: A Secret Life.* New York: Harper, 1998.

## Dorothy P. Miller

"Dorothy Miller." *Delaware Audubon.* delawareaudubon.org/about/board_bios/dmbio.html.

"Dorothy Miller." *Newark Charter School.* dcet.k12.de.us/teach/cyberfair/cornett/dmiller.html.

www.ingramcontent.com/pod-product-compliance
Lightning Source LLC
LaVergne TN
LVHW070239120826
845154LV00022B/140

* 9 7 8 0 9 7 9 3 3 5 0 8 2 *